"I so believe in Phil's ability, that I entrust
and celebrity to partner with him in my sk_
Essentials, for many years. Everything it became, happened
under Phil's watchful eye."

— Carol Alt, Supermodel, Author, Entrepreneur,
Raw Lifestyle Expert

"This book is a must read for marketers who want to learn how
to engage with their customers in the digital age. Phil has superb
ability and insight to identify great marketing opportunities.
Providing solutions over products is the way to build a long-
term relationship with your customers and Phil is providing
you with a roadmap."

— Bob Circosta – TV's Original Home Shopping Host
and "TV's BILLION DOLLAR Man"

"After working with Phil on multiple brand projects, I can
confidently say that he's a true original. Phil is a fearlessly
creative thinker, with forward-thinking ideas and enterprising
solutions. He's a fascinating entrepreneur, with fascinating
ideas."

Sally Hogshead, New York Times bestselling author of
Fascinate: How To Make Your Brand Impossible to Resist

"Phil has proven himself to be a creative thought leader and
driven manager who gets results."

Henry Nasella, LNK Partners

"Working with Phil for many years, I have found him to be a valuable thought leader in e-commerce and digital marketing."

Brad McGinity, Co-Founder, Windsor Circle Predictive Lifestyle Marketing

THINK ENGAGE THRIVE™

Marketing Actions To Skyrocket Your Brand In The Digital Age

Table of Contents

This book is dedicated to my lovely wife and son for supporting me and my growing list of ideas and endeavors.

Forward

I've been enabling technology to meet marketing goals my entire life. At least I thought I was until I met Phil Masiello. For as long as I can remember I've always had this strange chemistry that dances between left and right brain thinking. As my life, love, and career unfolded, I found myself at the helm of Unleashed Technologies deploying expert web technologies... that's how I met Phil.

A mutual friend, who had been working with Phil for some time, introduced us. Phil was in the middle of another wildly successful startup business he'd put together giving consumers exactly what they wanted when it came to subscription-based personal products. As our mutual friend introduced us, I knew just by interfacing with him that we had an opportunity for something special. Not because of just the work that Phil was bringing to our firm but how I knew he would challenge us to be better than we were the day before. He certainly didn't disappoint.

The next 2 – 3 years together were a whirlwind, and the teams of Unleashed Technologies learned so much from Phil and what mattered when it came to marketing that sometimes I wondered who should be paying who. Never afraid to speak his mind or help us be a better firm from our time working together many of the principles that he laid before us in being the best partner we could be still echoed in the hallways today. As a leader, I always went to Phil to find out how we were doing and how our teams were performing because of his ability to be rational, fair and understanding were unmatched. That's always been, Phil. Pushing hard, expecting results, and showing a passion for his peers, clients, and family. I'm truly honored and privileged to introduce "THINK ENGAGE THRIVE– Marketing Actions to Skyrocket Your Brand in the Digital Age".

This book helps cut through the clutter that can pollute the craft of marketing and help us remember the core principles and actions that are at the root of every successful brand and campaign. I'm proud to call Phil a mentor, and I can't say I'm surprised that's ended up in a book about helping other people.

Michael Spinosa
Chief Executive Officer Unleashed Technologies, LLC
http://www.unleashed-technologies.com

0 – "They All Have the Same Stuff"

For all my early life, food was a passion and a paycheck for me. My family owned an Italian restaurant, where I helped out any way I could. At age fourteen, I started learning to cook. My skills led to jobs at a lot of great places, some of them big names like Tavern on the Green and Maxwell's Plum. While I was in college, I studied under Albert Kumin, one of the greatest pastry chefs and chocolat iers there's ever been. I worked beside him for a year and a half, learning techniques that plenty of top chefs have never heard of. Well into my twenties, I thought my destiny was to buy a restaurant, where I'd divide my time between running the kitchen and greeting the guests, occasionally ducking into the office to put my feet up.

The thing is, as anybody in the industry can tell you, running a restaurant is tough, especially when you're first starting out. The hours are brutal, the stress nonstop. People will rob you blind if you're not on site constantly. That's why so many restaurants are run by families. That way, hopefully, Ma and Pa can take an afternoon off without locking up the till. The more I studied restauranteering, the less I liked my prospects for having a life outside of work. And I did want a life. That's why I decided to find a different way to earn my living.

Thanks to the training I'd had and connections I'd made, I was able to get a job working for Grand Union Supermarkets. This was not long after the company had been bought by Sir James Goldsmith, a British tycoon who wanted to create supermarkets like the great food halls of Europe. Instead of being limited to grocery fare, Goldsmith wanted his upscale shops to offer prepared foods, fresh pastries, and deli items to shoppers in high-end neighborhoods. He had a revolutionary vision, one that challenged the perception of what a supermarket in the US could be.

I was excited to get in on the ground floor. Our pilot stores in New Jersey had chefs making elaborate dishes. I spent a lot of time supervising operations and collecting feedback from customers face-to-face. People loved what we were doing, and they would sometimes ask about buying large quantities of food. One lady laid out a massive order, asking me for what amounted to dozens of pounds of fully prepared meals. I had to tell her we weren't set up for the kind of volume she was after.

It seemed strange to me that she would come to a grocery store, even a nice one, with such a request. So I asked her, "Why don't you go to a caterer?"

Her answer changed my life. "They all have the same stuff," she said. "Grilled salmon, stuffed chicken breast, heavy sauces. When you ask for customization, they don't give it to you. It's just terrible." She explained that she had parties at her house on a regular basis. I don't remember why—some library club she was involved in, or a charity.

Listening to her, it dawned on me that there was a huge unmet need for customized catering in the New York-New Jersey area. I had some friends who worked in catering, so I looked into what it would take to satisfy that need. What I found was that the big boys, the Silver Palates of the world, didn't want to customize. They provided a fixed menu, no choice involved. So I went to my friends and absorbed everything I could about the ins and outs of event catering. I'd mastered the skills of a food artisan. The chefs and instructors I learned from taught me to do amazing things. I thought, why not use my skills to go into business for myself?

So I did. After eleven years of cooking meals, waiting tables, doing pretty much everything in food outside of catching the fish or milking the cow, I decided to create a specialty food store and off-premises catering business. Weddings, museum events, and parties like my wealthy customer liked to host would be opportunities to show off my talents without having to work the grueling hours a restaurant required. I'd be able to put in a measly eight hours a day instead of the twelve to sixteen I'd been used to. Looking forward to this virtual vacation, I scouted a location. Plans came together quickly, and I soon opened The Fabulous Food Store and Catering in the suburbs around NYC.

The neighborhood was already well-known for crafts and antiques. Shoppers came down from the city every weekend to browse and bargain. Fabulous Foods was a welcome addition to the attractions. Everybody who came in was impressed by the customization we offered. In a short time, orders took off. I had to hire more staff to mind the store, work parties, drive trucks, and coordinate the work we were doing. Everything happened better and faster than I had planned, but I made one big mistake. I built so much of our brand around my personal knowledge and skills that recruiting became a major time sink. The food we offered was so specialized, so I couldn't just bring people off the street into my kitchen. Chefs and assistants had to meet a high standard. Providing their training killed my dream of working a nine-to-five.

Eventually, I moved on, but not before learning plenty about running a business. The most important takeaway was that when it comes to dealing with customer events – weddings, anniversary parties, or whatever – everybody wants theirs to be special, an expression of their personality. People love uniqueness, and that's what Fabulous Food gave them. By taking the time to THINK about what my customers loved, I'd been able to solve their problems in a way that nobody else was doing at the time. Providing solutions allowed me to ENGAGE with customers, establishing relationships that felt personal even when I never met the customer. Very quickly I came to realize that this process of thinking and engaging was what made my business THRIVE.

Since then, THINK ENGAGE THRIVE, has been at the heart of everything I've done. Thanks to the successes it enabled, I've built a career out of solving problems for customers. This approach benefited my employers, including Grand Union Supermarkets, Sutton Place Gourmet, and Harris Teeter. It helped me successfully launch my own retail businesses, among them The Daily Market, Raw Essentials, and 800Razors.com. And it's been vitally important to the clients I've served as an organic marketing expert, most recently in my role as Founder and CEO of Hound Dog Digital. Years ago, I observed that the maître d' of a high-class restaurant meets his guests' needs before they think to ask. In all the positions I've held, I've tried to do the same. Not every endeavor has taken me as far as I thought it could have, but I've exceeded projections more often than not. I've never walked away a loser.

Will THINK ENGAGE THRIVE work for you? I don't doubt it for a second. Whether you're a marketer looking to push your company to the next level or an entrepreneur looking to upset the status quo, THINK ENGAGE THRIVE is the formula you need to skyrocket your brand. What do I mean by skyrocket? In May of 2017, CNBC.com published their "Disruptor 50", a list of companies "whose innovations are changing the world."[1] The top 4 spots belong to companies who have used the power of mobile connectivity to innovate spaces in the real-world. Airbnb has done that for accommodations, Lyft and Grab have done it for transport, and WeWork has done it for small business real estate. These companies are a testament to the power of thinking outside the box, but they're also proof of the breakneck speed at which the Internet can help a company get off the ground. These brands didn't exist a decade ago, yet they have transformed their industries. With THINK ENGAGE THRIVE in your toolkit, nothing will stop you from doing the same.

It will take work. No business idea is a guarantee of overnight success. There are obstacles to be overcome and pitfalls to be avoided. We'll discuss some of them in detail later on. For now, just know that if you want your brand to take off, THINK ENGAGE THRIVE is your launch pad, your fuel, and your rocket engine. The disruptors I've just mentioned, as well as the examples I'll be using to illustrate future points, have all used some form of THINK ENGAGE THRIVE. It's not a concept I've pulled out the clear blue sky but a set of techniques that smart marketers have been using for years. They're what drive success in our data-rich age. By putting them to work for you, you can avoid the mistakes of

---

[1]https://www.cnbc.com/2017/05/16/the-2017-cnbc-disruptor-50-list-of-companies.html

many start-ups that never got off the ground, and established companies that sputtered and crashed for want of growth.

Your brand is a rocket. Marketing is the fuel. To get airborne, you need THINK ENGAGE THRIVE. Fueling up with its techniques will equip your company to reach new heights. To explain how it will add lift, let me first tell you what marketing is to me.

What Marketing Is (and What It Isn't)

The foundation of any successful business is knowing your customers—who they are and what they want. Thanks to the Internet, it's easier than ever to do that today. Search engines can tell you what's hot. Once you establish an online presence, data mining tools can tell you who's visiting your website, who's buying, and where they're coming from. Digging a little deeper, you can find out how your customers spend time online, unearth trends in their responses to your campaigns, and identify weaknesses in the competition. Through social media, you can reach out to customers where they live, connecting in ways that were impossible a few years ago. With so much data available, the question becomes, "What am I going to do with all this?"

As it turns out, that's not an easy question to answer. Part of the problem is that marketing is so widely misunderstood. To me, marketing is what you do to connect with customers so they'll buy your product. That's it. That's the definition that's worked for me since I started my first business at age twenty-five. It still works for me today. There's no reason to get more complicated than that, but academic types often do.

According to the American Marketing Association (AMA), *"Marketing is the activity, set of institutions, and processes for creating, communicating, delivering and exchanging offerings that have value for customers, clients, partners and society at large.²"* What does that mean? I have a master's in business administration, and after reading that definition forty-seven times, I still don't see how it can help you sell a product, offer a service, or grow your business. It's so nonspecific that you could apply this definition to practically any job where you're making something and it would work. Take shoe cobbling. *"[Shoe cobbling] is the activity, set of institutions, and processes for creating, communicating, delivering and exchanging [shoes]."* Change "shoe cobbling" to "woodworking," and "shoes" to "furniture" and the definition fits. Now, it's true that you can market shoes, furniture, and anything else you want to talk about, but nothing in the AMA's definition tells you where manufacturing ends and marketing begins.

Let's look at another attempt, this time by one of the thought leaders in the industry. According to Dr. Philip Kotler, *"Marketing is the science and art of exploring, creating, and delivering value to satisfy the needs of a target market at a profit. Marketing identifies unfulfilled needs and desires. It defines, measures, and quantifies the size of the identified market and the profit potential. It pinpoints which segments the company is capable of serving best, and it designs and promotes the appropriate products and services."³*

²https://www.cnbc.com/2017/05/16/the-2017-cnbc-disruptor-50-list-of-companies.html

"About AMA: Definition of Marketing," American Marketing Association, retrieved December 19, 2016, https://www.ama.org/AboutAMA/Pages/Definition-of-Marketing.aspx.

³"Dr. Philip Kotler Answers Your Questions on Marketing," Kotler Marketing Group, retrieved December 13, 2016, http://www.kotlermarketing.com/phil_questions.shtml.

"Science and art." "Delivering value." "Unfulfilled needs and desires." Dr. Kotler covers a lot of bases. The thing is, unless you're actually sitting in a classroom taking an exam based on his lectures, I can't imagine a person actually using this definition. It's overwhelming. If you think in terms of a corporation, you can clearly see why businesses get bogged down in meeting after meeting, endlessly recasting their strategy to capture a "science and art" such as Kotler describes. Entrepreneurs move faster than corporations partly because they don't have to care about definitions. When you move past overcomplicated definitions, you can expand your view to take in what marketing means in the real-world.

That's the essence of THINK ENGAGE THRIVE. Last chapter's comparison notwithstanding, marketing isn't rocket science. Fancy definitions for it fail because they obscure the simple truth behind all successful sales transaction. Marketing is what you do to connect with customers so they'll buy your product. People buy from you because you made a connection. Everything you do to make that connection is marketing. If you connect, you sell. Simple! So why do so many businesses fail in their marketing efforts?

One major reason is holding on to outdated marketing models. Fifty years ago, businesses rarely got the chance to take the pulse of a local market, much less a national or international one. Companies couldn't get to know their customers in ways that are commonplace today. Rather than thinking about customers, engaging with them, and thriving, marketers in that data-poor age concentrated on creating need – getting people to want what the company was equipped to sell. The success or failure of those efforts usually came down to how innovative the product was, or how rare. Selling

Bentleys back when they were the only cars with a lightweight aluminum engine, or selling Coca-Cola when the only competition was nameless, flavored soda water, didn't require a blockbuster campaign.

These days, launching a new product almost always means shouldering your way into a crowded market. The data-poor age is long over, so the models from that age don't work any more, if they ever worked at all. Take focus groups, for instance. It should come as no surprise to anyone that people lie. It turns out that when you bunch them up together, present them with a choice they mostly don't feel strongly about one way or the other, and prod them to give their opinion, they lie more, not less. This is not hard to understand.

Imagine being ushered into a room with a bunch of strangers. You're presented with a product to sample, asked to view an ad, or shown logos for a popular brand. A questioner, whom you could be excused for thinking of as your interrogator, asks you and others in the group questions about your habits and preferences. Make no mistake, brand preferences are deeply personal. We chose what we like based on the very observations and experiences that define us as individuals. None of us want to be judged for who we are. So when put we're put in a position where we have to express ourselves to a group, most of use will say anything but the truth. Who's going to reveal their deep, dark secrets in such a setting?

Companies that use focus groups don't think of preferences as deep and dark because they haven't thought through human nature. No opinion exists in a vacuum. It's part of our self-image. Say a questioner asks a lady in a focus group if she likes donuts. What's her thought process going to be? "Is this guy saying I'm fat? What about that skinny chick down there? Is he gonna ask her if she likes rice cakes?" Whatever answer she comes up with is going to be worthless to the company, if not downright destructive. Anybody who tells you they can build a successful campaign from what they heard in a focus group is either a fool or a con man about to try to sell you the Brooklyn Bridge.

Ask any woman if she prefers to buy natural, organic skin care products, and ninety-nine times out of a hundred she'll say yes. It sounds like a dumb question, right? Women in overwhelming numbers will tell questioners that natural products are what they want to buy. But the reality is, people who buy skin care products don't believe natural products get results. Companies have tried bringing 100% organic, natural skin care lines to market multiple times, yet none has been successful. In contrast, the use of injectable botulism, aka botox, and washes made from synthetically altered hyaluronic acid, is widespread. Customers can see, when they look at the results of using these products, that they rapidly erase fine lines and wrinkles around the eyes and lips. Who cares if they're riddled with poisons, artificial substances, and synthetically-altered compounds? If you listen to the data gathered from the focus group, where all these women say they want to buy 100% natural and organic products, it looks like the tail is wagging the dog here. But that's not the case. Actual buying figures show that artificial ingredients are the gold standard in the skin care business.

I've consulted for clients who've spent hundreds of thousands of dollars on focus groups and similar studies. In a few minutes on a computer, I've debunked the results they got using free tools. Don't waste time and money collecting lies. Focus groups won't tell you what customers do and love. As insidious as they are, though, there's another model of marketing from the data-poor age that hurts my brain even more – the 4Ps.

The 4Ps Aren't About Marketing

In this era of Amazon, markets are so saturated and consumers so inundated with brand choices that an industry has cropped up around unboxing stuff on YouTube. Think about that for a second. If the folks who make money reviewing products online barely have time to slice through the tape and give their opinion on the packaging, what does that say about the attention span of your customers? Simply this: People don't shop around for what they don't already love. Nobody's got that kind of time.

Back when I was an undergrad and again in grad school the 4Ps, was sold to me in the same way it's sold to thousands of marketing students every year, as our discipline's fundamental principle. As a comedy routine, this one kills me. But as a framework for selling in the real-world? I didn't buy the 4Ps when I was a student. After decades of professional experience, I can tell you that conclusively that the 4Ps aren't about marketing at all.

With their concentration on the eponymous Product, Price, Promotion, and Place, the 4Ps put focus on technology, not customers. There might be something redeemable about the model if it put emphasis on the differentiators that set a product apart, but the question of why is a customer going to be better off buying from me than a competitor is barely addressed in the 4Ps. Consider, for example, the difference between a cup of coffee at Dunkin' Donuts and a similar brew at Starbucks. Both companies sell a product called "coffee", but nothing in that bare fact suggests that a cup from one is preferable to a cup from another. Promotion might be expected to make that case to the customer; in reality, neither company centers their promotions around coffee. It's sold as an add-on at Dunkin'. At Starbucks, it's part of an experience package, alongside the soundtrack albums and breakfast sandwiches you see so attractively displayed. Place is irrelevant to the question of what sets each brand's coffee apart, given how easy it is to find both in cities and suburbs and just off the highway. What about price? It's true that the price of a Dunkin' Donuts coffee is significantly different from a similarly-sized coffee bought at Starbucks. However, for reasons I'm about to go into, any company pointing to a price as a key differentiator is quickly going to find themselves out of business.

Price doesn't win brand wars. If it did, Hilton would be only one hotel chain, McDonald's would be the only fast food, and Swanson would have the TV dinner section all to itself. At the end of the day, however deep you cut your margin, somebody can always turn out knock-offs of your product cheaper than you can put out the real deal. Consider Rolex. They're certainly not the only company who knows how to make a nice watch. If price was all that mattered, you'd expect Rolex to have been driven out of business decades ago. Yet their name is still synonymous with luxury all over the world. How did Rolex stay viable in a field of cheaper competitors? If you've ever shopped for a Rolex, you know it wasn't by lowering their prices. In fact, the Rolex brand image requires that they keep prices high. There's a small and very select group of companies that compete with Rolex, and none of them do it on price. Do you think if Cartier sent out a 20% off Groupon, all the Rolex customers would switch their allegiance? Of course not. Those folks are used to paying a premium for quality and the cachet that goes along with it. They're not going to be swayed by a price drop.

Luxury watches are marketed to a niche audience, true. But purchasing decisions on products from housewares to hamburgers are made in the exact same way. Customers have reasons outside of product, promotion, price and place for settling on a certain brand, and they generally stick with the brands they know until a company gives them a reason to change. Value can be that reason, but price is not the same as value. To estimate value, you have to look at the total impact a product has on a person's life. Price alone doesn't motivate people to part with their money. That whole concept is crazy, right? A customer would have to be dangerously unbalanced to buy a product that does nothing to meet their wants or needs, at any price.

Product, price, promotion and place don't make sales. As I mentioned earlier, being innovative will help a product sell, but even a one-of-a-kind gizmo can't sell itself. Customers look for features and buy benefits. Without a connection to the customer, marketers have no way to communicate features and benefits. As I saw time and again at my bespoke catering business, great companies solve problems for their customers. Customers, in turn, reward great companies with repeat sales. Successful marketing, therefore, involves about educating the customers on what solutions a company can provide. Where in the 4Ps is the customer? Nowhere. That's why I say the 4Ps aren't about marketing. They don't sell solutions and they don't inspire loyalty or repeat sales. Another word for repeat sales is retention. If you're a kid running a lemonade stand and you can only get one bag of lemons, maybe you don't care about retention. That's literally the only example I can think of where retention might not matter. Dunkin' Donuts, Starbucks, and all the other big name brands got where they are by knowing how to keep customers coming back.

I'll give you another example of a company that knows how to ENGAGE with repeat buyers: Amazon. They did a great job with the Dash button. If you don't know what that is, picture a keychain-sized piece of plastic with a brand name on it, like Tide or Peet's Coffee. Half the keychain is taken up by a button hooked up to your WiFi. You stick one of these things next to your washing machine or percolator and every time you're close to running out of whatever you need, you click the button to reorder. No trips to the supermarket or Walmart necessary, no reason to hunt down a sale. One press of the button, and two days later, a box shows up on your front porch. The Dash button is a double retention machine. It locks the customer into a brand—Tide, Peet's, whatever—and a retailer, Amazon. If you're ever looking for an example of a "win-win" to put in the dictionary, there it is.

How can you beat convenience like the Dash button? That's a serious question. Whoever brings a better way to market might as well have a license to print money. Here's the point. If you were an executive sitting in a marketing meeting at Amazon, and the marketing model you'd been taught was the 4Ps, something like the Dash button would look like a one-off gimmick at best. It's not much of a product. It says nothing about price. It's not a promotion, since you've got to get the buttons into people's homes before they start selling for you. The same can be said about place. It's only when you set aside the 4Ps that the brilliance of the idea starts to show through.

In the data-poor age, marketing textbooks could get away with stating the obvious, even the obviously wrong, because there wasn't enough data to call them on it. Yes, when you look at a successful marketing scheme you're going to see a product, with a price, being promoted, in a place. But now that we have empirical data about customer buying habits, it's time to dispense with the illusion that the combination of those factors even begins to touch on what marketing actually is. Marketing is what you do to connect with customers so they'll buy your product. Success in marketing requires that you THINK ENGAGE THRIVE.

The THINK ENGAGE THRIVE Cycle

The most important thing to remember when you're learning how to be a marketing success is that THINK ENGAGE THRIVE is a cycle. You don't THINK, then ENGAGE, then THRIVE, then promptly go out of business. Parsing out the component parts is often impossible and usually pointless. When you're getting set to launch a new marketing campaign, THINK will obviously happen first, since planning goes into everything you do. But you don't stop thinking at the moment you ENGAGE. In fact, your first sale should motivate you to THINK about what you did right and what you could have done better. Engaging is functionally synonymous with making a sale, so you don't want to stop doing that. Thinking helps you how to solve the customer's problem; engaging puts a smile on their face. Having planned well and executed effectively, you set your company up to THRIVE. But THRIVE is not the as the end of the cycle. Like a wheel, THINK ENGAGE

THRIVE goes round and round. Every success should make you ask how you can repeat your success, maybe use it to grow.

THINK ENGAGE THRIVE moves. It progresses. But it's not rocket science. It's mostly common sense, empathy, and a willingness to modify an approach based on customer behavior data. If we were to map out a real-world example, you'd see that thinking leads to engaging, engaging leads to more thinking, better thinking causes more engagement, and all this grows and sustains the business. The flow chart would look like a circuit, not a straight line. But just as a circuit relies on switches, there are points in THINK ENGAGE THRIVE where actions have happen in order for power to flow. These actions can be ordered as steps, though it's wrong to think of each step as executing only once, or always in the same order. Steps repeat, they overlap. Switch on THINK and ENGAGE charges up. Store enough current and ENGAGE sends a jolt back through THINK to light up THRIVE. If marketing was a jukebox, it'd always be on shuffle. If it was a pinball machine, every thousand points would drop a multi-ball, and scoring bumpers would give 500 points a pop.

There's no point talking around it: cycles are hard to understand. Steps, on the other hand, are easy. If for no better reason than to make THINK ENGAGE THRIVE easier to comprehend, here is a breakdown in the typical, first-run progression:

Step 1: Identify Your Customers

Step 2: Find Out What They Love

Step 3: Sell Them Solutions

Step 4: Run the Numbers

Step 5: Adjust Your Pitch

You'll notice I haven't labeled any one step as THINK or ENGAGE or THRIVE. In fact, I see elements of each in every step. Roughly, though, you can conceptualize THINK as taking in Steps 1 & 2, ENGAGE as governing Step 3, and THINK returning for Steps 4 & 5. Where's THRIVE, you ask? The basic formula is that THINK + ENGAGE = THRIVE, meaning that THRIVE is the result of your hard work. There's nuance here, though. When you THINK and ENGAGE, you generate capital, and that capital should help your company grow. If you want to make it in business, you have to play the long game. THRIVE is not the end of a company's journey. Rather, it's an opportunity to invest in future engagement opportunities, thinking along the way.

Let's make that a bit more concrete. Say you rent out space at a mall. You've got a machine that makes snow-cones. The first question you need to ask is, "How am I going to get people to buy my snow-cones?" Whatever answer you come up with is, by definition, your marketing. For your snow-cone business, marketing might mean dancing around in a cardboard cone while handing out samples to kids coming out of the movie theater. Your big, dopey suit costs $40. Fifty to a hundred snow-cones run you maybe $1.50 in syrup. Rent and electricity are routine expenditures, so they don't figure into the marketing budget. Time does, though, so say you spend ten minutes giving out product at six different showings per day, for a total of seven hours invested in the course of one week.

What steps have you covered so far? Clearly you put some thought into Step 1 – you identified kids as your customers. In fact you got more specific than that, realizing that kids who just watched a movie would be ready for a treat. Step 2 is easy. Kids love snow-cones. Reflecting back on Step 1 (which you can't help but do, since THINK ENGAGE THRIVE is a cycle) you realized that since kids don't generally have money, you'd have to make your product appealing to moms or dads or siblings, which you did by extending their rug rats' good mood. You completed Step 3, and moved on from THINK to ENGAGE, by putting yourself in the right place at the right time. In fact, you did something really special, solving problem your customers didn't realize could be solved. The movie was over, but you kept the fun going. How awesome are you?

Now it's time look at the numbers, in line with Step 4. Despite your added expenditures, your receipts show that this was your strongest week of snow-cone sales ever. You moved three times as many cones as your previous best week! How did that happen? From what you overheard, the kids who ate your promo cones told their friends about the "crazy cone guy" at the mall. Those friends came to see you ASAP, not at promo time, so they paid full price. More accurately, their parents did. It wasn't just the kids you managed to win over. Some financiers of the movie crowd told their friends how much fun the kids had. Those friends sought you out. They didn't mind paying a buck fifty for ten minutes of peace while they shopped for chinos. Your promotion sparked engagement with customers who weren't even present at the time. So, where do you go from here? Step 5 suggests you adjust your pitch. Obviously, if something's working, you should consider riding the train as long as you can. Maybe you should keep working the theater crowd, but don't stop there. Your first week of thriving means you've got more money to put into next week's promotion. Maybe you can add a new flavor to your syrup selection, or invest in a helium tank and some balloons.

During your second week, you notice that some of your repeat customers are ladies you've seen power-walking around the mall in the early morning, during the hour between when the mall doors open and the stores raise their gates. One of the department stores, an anchor at the mall, offers a daycare service for that hour. The space you rent is on the opposite end of the concourse from that anchor, and you're not allowed to start selling until the walking hour is over, so it's never occurred to you to target these ladies as customers. Now that you know they're interested, is there a way you can turn these limitations into an opportunity? The kids are bound to be hungry after running around for an hour. Could you do a deal with the anchor store to let you show up just as the walkers are heading out? The store is clearly interested in keeping their customers happy. If they don't bite, what about asking the mall owners to let you use the sidewalk outside?

Even the best campaigns can be improved by tweaking and adjustment. You don't want your customers getting bored with your message. The good news is, every success teaches you how to keep their attention. When you sell two hundred snow-cones a day, ask, "How can I sell two thousand? Twenty thousand? Two-hundred thousand?" Remember that THRIVE is not the end. Because THINK ENGAGE THRIVE is a cycle, you get to decide when a product, a product line, or an entire business has run its course. Until you make that call, every success will present you with a chance to double down on what's working, eliminate what's not, and try new ways to connect with your customers.

That's the basics – THINK ENGAGE THRIVE pared down to five iterative steps. Over the next five chapters, we'll explore how each step will help you skyrocket your brand. I'll provide examples drawn from my career as an entrepreneur and a marketing expert, highlight useful tools and present case studies illustrating how you can be successful as a marketer in the data-rich age. Due to the cyclical nature of THINK ENGAGE THRIVE, you will see crossover, one step bleeding into another. As you come to understand the principles behind the concepts we discuss, you'll come to appreciate the freedom this enables.

1 – Identify Your Customers

When does a person become a customer? Think about that for a minute. The word "customer" implies "custom", in the old-fashioned sense of doing business with somebody. Does money have to exchange hands before you can say that you've done business? For our purposes, I'm going to say, "No." A customer, in the sense I'll use the term, is anybody who can benefit from a product. They're a person with a problem, the solution to which can be bought and sold. Identifying your customer is really an exercise in targeting. You're trying to narrow down the person or group of people who can benefit from the solution your company provides. This maximizes your marketing efficiency, allowing you to do more for less. We live at a time when it's possible to send a personalized email to practically anybody you want to, anywhere on the globe. There's no excuse not to know who wants your products.

Of course, just knowing isn't enough. You've got to be prepared to use what you know. With more than sixteen years in food retail, I can tell you that one thing every supermarket should know is who their customer is. After all, they've been collecting vital data about shopping habits since the mid-90s. Every time you flash a discount card at Harris Teeter, Publix, Piggly Wiggly, or Mayfair, you're adding to their cache of knowledge. Their databases remember the time you came in for hamburgers, then had to return an hour later to buy buns. They know how quickly you run out of dishwashing liquid and your preference for hypoallergenic detergent. But what do the companies do with this information? Very little and not nearly enough. Why? Because supermarkets don't know how to sell.

What most shoppers don't realize about the grocery business is that big stores make their money buying products, not selling product. They focus on vendors who pay for the privilege of slotting their goods in the store. Opening up space to a vendor is what turns profit for them. Most supermarket buyers have become accountants. Because of this institutional apathy, most grocery chains don't use the tasty data they've been hoarding for so many years. This leaves them stuck in outdated, broken marketing models like the 4Ps. They're starving at a feast! Not knowing who their customer leaves supermarkets vulnerable. That's the major reason why a host of non-traditional stores like Aldi and Trader Joe's, plus mega-retailers like Walmart, and nao Amazon, have been able to move in on their territory in recent years. How, exactly, does a traditional supermarket operate?

Suppose I'm selling a value brand of dental floss. The product costs $1 to make, package, and deliver. I have to turn a profit, so I offer it wholesale for $1.50. A supermarket buyer agrees to meet me to discuss selling in his chain's one hundred stores. The buyer likes my product because its price point fills a gap between the store brand and Oral-B. So he wants to buy, only he says the store's going to need $10,000 up front to slot my product in their warehouse. This is a per-product fee, mind you. If I come out with a mint version of my floss, I'll have to negotiate a separate fee. In addition, the store requires a 10% rebate on all sales for one week a month, so they can run promotional prices. Space in the circular, which is mandatory, starts at $5,000 per quarter. Also, I'm going to need to hire a broker whose people will do the actual stocking and assemble in-store displays.

"That's all par for the course," says the buyer, "and speaking of which, we'll expect you to buy a foursome in our golf tournament for the March of Dimes. That'll run another $5,000 annually." He sticks me with the tab for our business lunch, then schedules a follow-up meeting in three months, suggesting we hit the new Japanese steakhouse across town.

If this sounds like a racket to you, that's because it it. Adding all my expenses together, I find that my cost is now $1 times number of units, plus 10% for the rebate, plus a 4% broker fee, plus $20,000 for four circulars, plus $10,000 for slotting, plus $5,000 in charity, plus (and I'm not kidding here) another $1,000 for booze-and-schmooze dinners. I do the math, estimating I can spread the additional cost over 100,000 units in the first year. That means I have to raise my sale price to the retailer by sixty cents just to cover these added costs! It's a sure bet that this isn't the end of the adjustments I'll have to make, and I can't afford to be optimistic, so I set wholesale at $3.00 and hope I can compete. The store sells my floss at $4.20 a unit. The $1.20 they could make per unit is small potatoes, in their minds, because the company has already made $36,000 buying product from me. I've incentivized them to take stock off my hands, not to get my floss into the baskets of their customers.

Contrast that with Walmart, where I could walk in the door at $1.50 per unit. Walmart would ask if shipping was included in that number. We'd negotiate for their trucks to pickup my floss, enabling me to drop the price by 5%. They'd go back and forth with me, finding all the ways I could save money, dropping the price as low as it can go. They'd make a commitment to buy half a million units. The only fee they'd assesses would be a 2% warehouse damage deduction. Ultimately, I'd be in a position to sell to them at $1.30 per unit. They'd collect their 500,000 units, price my floss at $2.50 a spool, and sell through every container, collecting a 48% margin. Everybody would be happy – Walmart with their profit on the sale, me with my $150,000 share of that profit, and Walmart's customers with the great deal they got on floss. The only exception would be the supermarket buyer, who would call me up furious, insisting that Walmart is selling my floss so much cheaper, I must be ripping him off.

Deals like this one aren't the exception, they're the rule for the supermarket industry. What they illustrate is the importance of focusing on your customer. Supermarkets typically behave as if vendors are more important than end users, which is stupid, since it's the promise of high customer sales that brings vendors to the table in the first place. In so doing they leave openings for customer-focused retailers like Walmart to eat their lunch. On some level, the supermarkets know this, but like an oil tanker, the industry continues to go the wrong way because it would take too much energy to turn around.

When a business doesn't focus on customers, it loses direction. It can't plot a course because it's set goals it's not equipped to reach. It pursues alternate sources of revenue, like the fees we've just discussed, because its primary sources are stagnating. This quickly leads to a feedback loop of bad decisions further weakening the customer-facing side of the business. For example, twice in my working life when I've been involved with food retailers who allowed individual stores, selling under their brand, to make decisions about which products would be carried on store shelves. Talk about losing focus on the customer! If a customer knows your brand, they expect a certain experience when they enter one of your stores. A major part of that experience is product assortment. Allowing a manager carte blanche to set their own planogram says to the customer that you don't know who they are or what they're coming in for. You're not going to make their shopping experience easy or convenient for them by consistently offering what they want, so why should they bother coming in at all? The brand confusion created by policies like this can erode customer loyalty to the point where it doesn't exist.

The first time I saw this in action was while working with a transition team for a supermarket chain that had just changed hands. Under the previous ownership, the president of the company had implemented a program of local managers setting their own merchandise. The board of directors realized that this was a bad idea and fired the president. Unfortunately, cutting off the head didn't solve the problem. We got complaints from folks at all levels, including managers who saw our unifying initiative as a power grab. To move forward, we quickly realized, we needed more than a change in policy. We needed to win over hearts and minds.

Convincing the doubters proved easier said than done. Even when we showed them that their methods were underperforming, some managers stuck to their guns. Our team had to shift personnel from one store to another so that the managers could see that there was a better way. Some couldn't hack it. They quit and went to work for our competitors, only to find that the changes we'd introduced were industry standard. The brain drain hurt the company for a time but it was worth it. In the end, sales went up, foot traffic went up, profit went up. Those folks who had stuck it out during the transition saw fatter bonuses and a rise in their personal stock.

My second encounter with this form of brand confusion happened when I was advising a regional convenience store chain. This time, the situation didn't turn out so well. As with the supermarket chain, each store under the chain's brand took a different approach to ordering and merchandising their stock. What made matters worse was that in this case, the company trusted the job of figuring this stuff out to remote operators who had little to no information about conditions on the ground.

I quickly discovered that much of the suffering came down to a corporate culture in which everybody made excuses. Every year the company did a comprehensive survey of store performance, and every year, the biggest customer complaint was, "I can't find what I come in to buy. Store A is always out of stock. Store B hides what I want behind the toilet paper. Store C doesn't even sell what I'm after." Every year the same complaint, yet nobody did anything about it. "Betty knows what sells in her store," they'd say. Maybe Betty did, but she didn't know what would have sold if she had taken the time to do her job right.

In an effort to plug leaks in the company dam, the team visited a store in Hoboken, NJ. It was an outstanding location, just one block away from the subway into NYC. Two doors down was a Dunkin' Donuts, home to my dark, decaf mistress. As I walked up to the convenience store, I could see racks of magazines and books in the window. The coffee and convenience foods had been moved to the back of the store. Now, if you're from a major city like New York, or even if you've just visited and paid attention to what was going on, you'll know that city dwellers don't look up at signs. Native New Yorkers don't look up at much of anything, in fact. The skyline's for tourists, that's why you see it on postcards. City dwellers look straight ahead, so they tend to decide what kind of store they're passing by looking in the windows. Ask yourself, "If I were walking by a shop that displayed magazines and books behind the glass, what would I think they were selling?"

As a brand, coffee and sandwiches were the company's big sellers. The store in Hoboken was struggling to move even the basic items. I told the operators to move the news rack to the back and get the food up front. Rather than listen, they came up with an excuse as to why they couldn't sell coffee at that store. The theory went like this: "Commuters into the city don't want to risk scalding themselves while riding the train, so they wait to buy their coffee on the other side."

As a New Yorker myself, I knew this was total bull. So I said to the manager, "I notice there's a Dunkin' Donuts two doors down. Are they busy in the morning?"

"Oh yeah," the manager said. "Cars are double-parked all up and down the street with people grabbing coffee before the train."

I looked at the operators and told them they should go to Dunkin' and explain their theory. After detailing the lessons learned from this trip to the CEO, I tried to get across the importance of brand consistency and execution. A slight change in policy, a unified merchandising plan, and their stores could have exploded. But the CEO wanted none of it. The store in Hoboken closed soon afterward, and I got the boot. I was told I didn't fit in with the brand's corporate values. Darn right I didn't! Complacency, excuses, and laziness were not qualities I wanted to rub off on me.

Useful Tools: Google Trends and Google Correlate

Recognizing the importance of putting the customer first is your first step to success. But you can't please everybody, right? In order to sell to your customer, you've got to know how to pick that customer out of the crowd. What do people who are going to be interested in your product have in common? Where can position your advertising so you can reach them effectively? Knowledge of your industry and common sense will help you narrow down your target. Knowing what's popular, what's trending, is also a major help. Enter Google Trends.

Trends is the first of three essential tools in what I call the Holy Trinity of Google. And it's great. If you want to know what topics are getting traffic today, you can find out in seconds by pulling up Google Trend's Top 20. You can filter these by category and/or country. With a bit of experimentation, you can drill pretty deep, unearthing patterns that will really help you know where the buying public's head is. Trends also lets you see how search terms have performed over time. For instance, did you know that from 2004 through 2016, "gift for boyfriend" was searched more often than "gift for girlfriend" on Google, but "gift for wife" trounced "gift for husband" in the same period? That may seem like a trivial example, but what does it suggest about how the chocolate industry is faring relative to consumer electronics? If you happened to be a jewelry importer, or an online content provider getting ready to launch a new sports package, knowing who's shopping for whom would have a major impact on next quarter's plans. You've got to look beyond the immediate to spot opportunities. That's what thinking outside the box is all about.

Not long ago, I was advising a tea company that specializes in hard-to-find imported teas. They were a relatively new company who naturally wanted to get the best bang for their advertising buck as the holidays rolled around. Before coming to me, they'd been emphasizing the nutritional advantages of certain varieties they had on offer. I was skeptical about this approach, and sure enough, when I checked historic holiday searches on Google Trends, I found that that "health benefits of matcha" doesn't attract any more special interest around this time. Gift-related searches, on the other hand, see a major upswing and searches for "stocking stuffers" and "gifts under $20" go off the chart. After showing these trends to my client, I recommended that we work together to assemble a promotional package highlighting a limited-time variety pack of popular teas, and another featuring and their loose leaf starter kits. The client was pleased. With a little simple Googling, I'd spared them from wasting money on a "Get Fit for Christmas" campaign. Instead, they dialed in on who their customers were and what problems they had that the company could help solve.

Once Google Trends starts you down the right path, you can do more analysis of trends over time using Google Correlate, which graphs search terms with similar incidences over a given period of time. Born out of a hypothesis that search trends on symptoms might be useful in predicting cases of flu, Correlate can show you patterns you might not expect. Searching "loose leaf tea" on Correlate is highly likely to tell you the leader in loose leaf tea retail in the selected time frame, since many people will search product type along with brand. But would it surprise you to know that the search incidence of "loose leaf tea" matched the search incidence for "crochet hook" 94.53% of the time in 2010? This doesn't mean that the same people who searched tea also searched hooks, but it's a curious enough coincidence to make me wonder. Can you picture your grandma sipping tea while she stitches you a sweater? If so, maybe, an experimental cross promotion isn't such a crazy idea.

Correlate offers aggregation on a week-by-week and month-by-month basis. Changing our "loose leaf tea" correlation search to monthly reveals commonality with searches for "roasted pork". A quick standard Google search uncovers several recipes incorporating these ingredients. Is there an opportunity for bundling spice packs? The term "get wax" also corresponds closely to the monthly "loose leaf tea" search incidence. Tea and aromatherapy candles sounds like a winning combination. I'm less convinced that "changing headlights", a search terms that closely correlates with "loose leaf tea" when viewed both monthly and weekly, is a natural fit. Sometimes a cigar is just a cigar.

Still, wise marketers ignore these high-tech insights at their peril. Google Trends shows a growing interest in soup recipes from December through January, followed by a leveling off in February, then a drop in March. Soup is dead to Google in the summertime. What, no gazpacho? Armed with this knowledge, you'd expect food retailers to build their soup ads around what customers are doing. When the weather got cold, they'd put soup on sale, beating out the competition. Yet I've seen supermarket fliers offering half-price gelato in January. That might make sense to a warehouse manager with limited freezer space, but from the marketing perspective, all it does is waste paper. Worse, it's a failure to THINK about customers and a missed chance to ENGAGE. Data tools like

Google Trend and Correlate make it easy to position yourself where customers want you to be, but only if you act on what they show.

Buyer Personas

So let's start acting! Once you have an idea about who wants to buy your company's solution, the next thing to make sure of is that everybody else in your company has the right outlook. And I do mean everybody, not just the marketing team. From CEO to office assistant, your company needs to conceptualize customers as individuals, each with their own wants and needs. Successful companies get specific about this. They talk about their customer the way you'd talk about a good friend, a family member, or your boss. Using data tools, they find out everything the Internet can tell them about specific customers, then boil down what they learn into a set of distinguishing traits. These traits go much deeper than census data, the source of demographics. They identify brand preferences on a variety of products, involvement in social and political movements, hobbies, and a dozen more granular characteristics. Marketers assemble these traits into mashups of a company's ideal customer. We call such a mash up a company's buyer persona. No matter the size of your company, a buyer persona can elevate your marketing plan.

Say you're looking to sell a new, distinguishably different type of watch. You've decided to focus on the young, urban, professional market, since that's the segment with the kind of income that could support a unique, semi-luxury product like yours. You ask yourself, "Who is my yuppie customer? What do they do?" Google will give you the basic demographics.

Picture men and women, college graduates, between the ages of 25 and 35. They have mid-level management jobs, tend to be creative, and like to go out to listen to music on the weekends. These are pretty good details to get your started. They tell you where your marketing might be effective – cabs over subways, GQ over AARP magazine – and suggest music websites as partners to support your digital presence. What they don't give you is confidence that yuppies are into watches. Is "young, urban professional" specific enough for your customer?

If you take a step back, you'll realize it's not. Yuppies in general are not your customers. Purchasing data across that demographic shows that most upwardly mobile types are concerned about their image. They do splash out on technology and fashion, but tend to be risk-averse when it comes to making choices that might mark them as different them from their peers. THINK a little deeper and you'll see that your customers are actually hipsters. Hipsters are people who are comfortable being trendsetters, who get excited about taking a chance on a new brand. Hipsters actively avoid the mainstream, since their goal is to be the first to appreciate the social, aesthetic, and ironic value of the tragically uncool. If you want your new watch brand to take off, it's hipsters you're going to have to get to light the fire that ignites your rocket fuel.

Search "yuppie watches", and you'll see brands like Seiko, Citizen, and Tag Heuer. Googling "hipster watches" turns up no established hipster timepiece, at time of writing. That itself should tell you that a) there is an opportunity here and b) yuppies and hipsters are not alike in tastes. How do you distinguish between the two? Originality is a hipster virtue, so unearthing traits common to hipsters takes work, but it definitely can be done. Ask a hipster what music he listens to and he's likely to list obscure indie rock bands with at least one member who plays an object that is not an instrument. Ask her if the last movie she saw was any good and she'll say, "Of course not. It was revolting. I'm attending the retrospective tonight." Any man with a beard, sleeve tattoos, and pants rolled up to mid-shin is probably a hipster. A woman with the same? She's their queen.

Okay, that last one's tongue-in-cheek, but the rest are not inaccurate. Hipsters resist classification. Go to the data, though, and you'll start to get what they're about. Many hipsters are vegan. Almost all will voice their support for social causes and left-leaning politics. They like bikes. Hipsters tend to see popular culture as something to be turned away at the door. They don't want to be seen as doing anything because of peer pressure or tradition. The trends they do embrace are intended to force observers out of complacency, to make them think. Because they're actively trying not to dress conventionally, their outfits tend to combine casual re-interpretations of formal wear with neatened-up grunge. They eat well, drink well, and leave a small carbon footprint. I'll leave discovering more traits as an exercise for the reader, but based on this list, I'm ready to build the buyer persona.

I always start with a name. This immediately gets me thinking about a living, breathing human being, with all the complexity and contradictions that involves. Since we're selling a gender-neutral watch, we'll actually need two names, two personas. Let's call ours Hipster Josh and Hipster Mary. Take a minute to fix their image in your mind. Hipster Josh is in his mid-twenties, bearded, with arm ink visible as he unbuttons his flannel cuffs. A spray of tightly braided, beaded hair spills out from under Hipster Mary's derby hat as she tilts her chin and adjusts John Lennon glasses. You see them now? Make sure, in your imagination, that Hipster Josh and Mary's wrists are visible. They've both been missing appointments, lately, and though they both have smartphones, they don't like to pull them out in public. They have a timepiece problem, one you can solve.

Now that you know what they look like, it's time to share their visual with the rest of the company. If you're not a graphic artist yourself, don't worry. The image you use doesn't have to match what you came up with in your head. It's an essence you're after. Clip photos from a magazine. Pull images from the Internet. Try to find a fashion model whose look suits what you're after – it's easier to Google if you know the model's name. Once you've got something that works, use Photoshop to locate your images in settings hipsters frequent – kava kava bars, anywhere with recumbent bicycle access. Email the result to everyone in the company. Print pictures out and post them in the halls. Your goal is to help everybody put faces to your buyer personas. Faces make us feel like we know somebody. That's why some blind people ask to feel your face when you meet them for the first time. You want everybody in your company to know Hipster Josh and Hipster Mary. You want them working everyday to anticipate Josh and Mary's needs.

Buyer personas really do make it easier for everybody on your team to communicate the company message. Demographics are cold, isolating. Companies that rely on them are compelled to refer to their customers in dehumanizing terms. They market to "men 18-34" or "women over 50". And you can't get to know a demographic. At best, they let you picture a crowd of faces with about the right hair and amount of wrinkles. You tell me. Is it easier to sell a great product to a friend you know will love it, or a stranger who's about the same age? If you care at all about your friends, I already know your answer. Don't stop at broad generalizations. Use buyer personas to get to know your customers.

Thinking about all the companies I've worked with over the years, the one that stands out as the best example of treating customers as individuals is Home Shopping Network. Former CEO Mindy Grossman put HSN's focus squarely on their buyer persona in every meeting I ever attended with her as chair. All suggestions at those meetings were put in terms of what the customer would like. Many times I heard sentences like:

"She wouldn't like us time shifting her favorite half-hour."

"She'd love to see this in spring colors."

"I know she'll eat up that product line."

The speakers weren't talking about Ms Grossman. The "she" in question was the customer. We all had to know who "she" was, personally. We got in the mindset of running everything by "her", our unseen boss. At HSN, the buy-in was great! It went from top to bottom, without gaps. During all the time I worked closely with HSN, "she" ruled all. Everybody worked hard to keep "her" happy. As a result, HSN functioned as a finely tuned machine. Compare that to the frustration companies go through when marketers, R&D, and fulfillment aren't on the same page. When companies don't focus on the customer, opinions on how to do business drift apart. Companies fracture, and it becomes tough to get anything done. Demographics alone can't fix this. Numbers don't motivate. People do.

When you pin up your photos of Hipster Josh and Hipster Mary and start talking about them as real people, your fellow watchmakers will fall in line. They'll talk the talk and walk the walk. Their time and yours will be spent doing the most good. And that's a wonderful thing. A company that truly knows its customer is like a rocket at full power, glorious to behold.

Case Study – Giant Food vs. Wegmans

Big chain supermarkets work on a real estate convenience model. I've already explained one reason customer happiness isn't their number one concern. Another is their faith that no competitor is going to do their job well enough that customers will bother driving a few extra miles to shop someplace else. In my area, a supermarket called Giant Food has a store that was doing about $900,000 in sales per week. Your average grocery store, like Kroger or Safeway, sells about one-third as much. This Giant wasn't fancy. They just happened to be in a location that did high volume. The store itself had done – and I'm being charitable here – very little to deserve its success. When Wegmans, a megastore out of Rochester, broke ground on a new location up the street, Giant got greedy. They immediately started remodeling their store, adding a variety of features.

Why do I say greedy? Weren't they just looking to compete? I'm sure they'd have made that argument, but it would have been a blind one. The services they were adding were just the sort of thing customers would have enjoyed having all along. You would have thought if Giant Food knew who their customers were and cared about making them happy, they would made these changes long ago. The key to understanding why they finally did is the fact that a typical supermarket draws customers from a two- to three-mile radius. But people love Wegmans. They go out of their way to shop there. So, a Wegmans can draw from a radius above twenty miles. What made Giant get on the ball was their realization that the new Wegmans would bring a lot of traffic to their area. The improvements were a ninth-inning play to preserve their image before their customer-focused competitor arrived to show them up.

Unfortunately for Giant, they couldn't compete, even after expensive upgrades. These days, that same stores does less than $200,000 in weekly sales. Wegmans, on the other hand, did $2.2 million in sales on week one, and since has grown to doing nearly three million. What does Wegmans get that Giant doesn't? That you have to know your customer. Wegmans is one of the precious few supermarkets that pays attention to their customer data. By examining it, they've figured out a secret about what customers want when they shop for groceries. It's not a hidden kind of secret. It just requires companies to THINK. They have to ask themselves, "What problem are customers looking to solve when they shop for food?" It's not, "The price of chicken's too high." When Shopper Steve strolls into a Giant or a Wegmans, he's thinking, "What am I going to put on the table tonight?" Steve's problem isn't price. It isn't even food. It's meals.

Every Wegmans store is structured around preparing meals. They have a deli, a café, a bakery, and a sandwich shop. At all these locations, customers can pick up meals on the go. Wegmans offers a kosher selection, a rotisserie area, even an Asian hot food bar. Giant tried to imitate some of these features, but because they were stuck in a vendor-focused, real estate convenience mindset, they didn't notice (or failed to implement) the innovations that let Wegmans go a step beyond. As you walk through a Wegmans, every department guides you into transforming food they sell into complete meals. Everything on the Wegmans website is oriented around this concept. Wegmans even distributes a free magazine in their stores with recipes you can pull together right off the shelves.

Features like these make shopping at Wegmans exhilarating. Customers feel like they're accomplishing a vital task. When they leave the store, it's with a sense that they've gotten a leg up on the daily grind. Wegmans creates this sense by applying customer data to every stocking and design decision. Their focus on serving customer needs builds loyalty and gets new folks in the door. They do a great job of thinking and engaging. No wonder they THRIVE.

Honestly, the contrast between their approach and what traditional supermarkets are stuck doing is not hard to get your head around. Yet the traditional chains continue to operate as if monthly rebates are all they have to offer to keep their customers hooked. They haven't yet learned the lesson that being cheap is not the same as being the best value. When I was working as CEO, Head Chef, and Whipping Boy of The Fabulous Food Store and Catering, I found out that because we were offering quality food and a unique menu, we could charge clients any price we wanted and they would pay. People didn't haggle when you're selling them products and services they can't buy anywhere else.

It's amazing to me that old-model supermarket chains are still able to keep their doors open, but don't let their continued existence fool you. Existing is not thriving, and many companies that look solid from the outside are in crisis mode now that innovative new players like Wegmans have entered the field. Lack of choice was a problem supermarket customers had to deal with for decades in many places. With an increasing number of solutions on offer, plenty of chains are going to find themselves choking on the exhaust of retailers who know how to skyrocket a brand.

2 – Find Out What They Love

Knowing who your customer is opens a path to ENGAGE. Maybe this is through ad messages on social media. Maybe it's in print or on TV. Whatever the case, what's important is that your message is getting out there in the best way to connect with customers. Customers don't like to be hard sold. They don't want marketers in their face yelling, "Buy this now!" Heavy-handed tactics are why so many major brands fail on social media. What customers like is learning about products that meet their needs, that provide solutions to their problems. Customers want to be served, and they'll support sellers who serve them through communication and education.

There are several companies who do a great job finding out what their customers love and messaging them in ways that keep them coming back. In this chapter, we'll talk about one of the most famous examples, Apple. I'll share a couple of tools that you can use to expand your knowledge of the customer, concentrating on generating keywords that will optimize your online ads. We'll discuss the difference innovation makes, then compare and contrast Apple with one of their faded competitors in our case study. You're going to see retention discussed at several points in this chapter. When people first set out to build a business, there's a tendency to think no further than the first big splash. Getting your name out in the twittersphere is important, sure, but social media is a fickle beast. If you can't back up your messaging, a single splash is all you're going to get. One day of trending won't make you a retail success. Engagement in marketing means keeping your finger on the customer's pulse and doing everything you can serve them over the long haul.

"Go to the Apple Store"

Apple has made amazing achievements in customer retention. What is it about the tech titan that makes folks stick with them for life? One major factor is education. How many times have you overheard an elderly person saying they'll never get the hang of a new piece of technology? It's a stereotype that shows up regrettably often in real life. Apple has proven that it doesn't have to be that way. They created the Apple Store not to sell product, but to educate their customers. Just look at the numbers. Renting and renovating and staffing and stocking hundreds of brick-in-mortar stores has been an expensive proposition for Apple. According to industry analyst Horace Dedidu, they spent in the neighborhood of $8.5 million to launch each of 220 stores over a five-year period starting September, 2005.[4] Yet at the time of this writing, physical stores account for less than 32% of Apple's total sales. The lion's share of Apple sales – 68% – happen online. To a less innovative company, making such a huge investment just to keep people interested might seem crazy, but Apple has demonstrated the value of customer loyalty time and time again. The "Geniuses" in Apple stores earn their pay not by selling, but by inspiring customers to value the company.

I got to see this up close when I bought my own dear mother an iPad some years ago. Mother wouldn't like me telling her age, but it's safe to say that by the time Reaganomics rolled around, she'd pretty much seen it all. Recent innovations in mobile technology might as well be something from another world, to hear her tell it. So when she looked at the tablet's

[4]Dedidu, H. (2011, October 14). How much does an Apple store cost? Retrieved September 19, 2017, from http://www.asymco.com/2011/10/14/how-much-does-an-apple-store-cost/

glossy touch screen, she felt intimidated. She told me she was too old to learn to use my gift.

I'd anticipated this, so I had my answer ready. I said, "Go to the Apple Store."

Mother's nearest location happened to be in a mall, which was a bonus. She likes to go to the mall in the middle of the day, when nobody is around but folks her own age. So when she showed up to ask about her iPad, she was surrounded by older people like her who got iPads from kids like me. All of a sudden, her trip became a social event! The store Geniuses did a great job interacting with their senior students. What could have been a nightmare experience for Mother turned into a fun outing she'd be glad to repeat. The training she received redeemed my extravagant gifting. Instead of her iPad becoming a white elephant, Apple's commitment to education ensured that it took on genuine value in her life. Understand, Mother is a sharp lady. She knew what the company was doing, how they were setting her up as a return shopper. And that was fine with her. She appreciated the help she got and she left happy, knowing that the next time she had a question, getting answers would be no problem. Now and forever, she'll be an Apple customer.

Here's an even more personal example. I'm a coffee fanatic. I orbit Dunkin' Donuts, touching down several times every day. The servers at my local shop all know me. As soon as I pull up to the drive-thru, they get an extra large decaf, no sugar, ready to put in my hand. I absolutely love their service. That and the consistency of their product elevates the brand to the next level. As I've already hinted, I admire Starbucks. Their quality, attention to detail, and service is top notch. But

I can't drink twelve tall decafs from Starbucks a day. Never mind the money, who's got that kind of time? The lines at Starbucks are killer. But I can drink twelve decaf Dunkies a day. The product and the way it's sold solves a problem for me. Sure price is a factor, but it's the engagement with my needs as a customer that keeps me coming back.

It comes down to this: A business that engages thrives; a business that doesn't dies. Apple and Dunkin' Donuts understand this. Despite the logistical gap that exists between high technology retail and mass market food service, both companies have an appreciation for customer loyalty in common. They understand that to continue to ENGAGE, they have to dig deep into what customers love. In Apple's case, their ultra-modern physical stores have helped countless seniors step into the digital age, while simultaneously meeting the needs of yuppies, soccer moms, and a dozen other buyer groups. Apple's broad appeal doesn't mean they lack focus. In fact it means the exact opposite. Rather than appeal to a sub-set of the population, they've found away to cut across lines, identifying qualities that are likely to draw customers to their brand, then actively supporting the expansion of those qualities. Dunkin' Donuts follows a similar strategy, using their dedicated locations to popularize their brands. When fans see the DD logo in supermarkets, say, or at a gas station, they get a warm, fuzzy feeling, a favorable glow brought on by memories of good experiences they had in the past.

Bringing in a wide variety of customers requires time and money. It's not always possible for a startup or a company still making a name for itself to attract a diverse clientele. That's why it's so important to identify your customers, then move beyond mere identity to find out what they love. Finding that out, then refining your approach in appreciation of customer needs is a never-ending process. Plans must always be fluid. Markets change over time. You have to be ready to change along with them.

Useful Tools: Google AdWords and Follow.net

If you're just starting out, how do you find out what your customers love? The basic answer is that you put yourself in the customer's place, analyze trends that tend to run in parallel with their interests, and experiment to find out what works best. This is where we get back to the cyclical nature of THINK ENGAGE THRIVE. You have to try out what you think will work first, keeping in mind all you know about the customer. Then you run the numbers. If your idea is a hit, you keep doing it. If it's a miss, you take a step back, reflect, adjust your pitch. Since every attempt you make is going to impact the company in major ways, you obviously want to bring your "A" game. You want to go out with your best ideas, trying experiments that have the best chance of a positive outcome. As the business grows, maybe you'll get into a position where it makes sense to try riskier ventures. At all times, you'll want to work with the best tools available.

A huge help in this area is Google AdWords. I'm mentioning it second in my Holy Trinity of Google, but it's actually the tool I use the most. AdWords is absolutely essential if you're running a pay-per-click (PPC) campaign. Even people who don't know what AdWords is see it in action all the time. After they visit a site that sells angora sweaters, suddenly they start seeing ads for sweaters pop up everywhere they go online. Every reference to "wool" or "winter" on CNN.

com gets linked back to the site they visited or to a competitor. It's uncanny how fast these targeted ads can come to dominate your web browsing experience, though background algorithms keep the rotation diverse.

Exactly what's going on in those algorithms is a Google trade secret, but in essence, when you show interest in a product online, AdWords remembers that interest and searches its database for participating advertisers who offer relevant content. Google defines "relevant" largely in terms of what an advertiser has bid to pay on a cost-per-click (CPC) basis, but a number of other factors are considered. These factors are bundled into the ad's Quality Score, and while the formula for QS is subject to change, it's not impossible to get a good idea of what Google looks at by examining the ranking of ads.

The sites that get linked on page margins and articles are enrolled in Google's partner program to AdWords, Google AdSense. AdSense pushes out the custom ads in sizes and locations determined by the site owners. Members also have some control over the type of ads they show – they can block out adult content, for instance – but within the context of what the site allows, the ads themselves are determined by Google's code. They don't stop at creating links in member content, of course. When you search for "Gillette Fusion Razors," Google gives you a scroll box filled with ads inviting you to buy razors from Target, Walmart, or others, plus manufacturer ads from Gillette itself. This is Google's Product Listing Ads. You can instantly compare prices and turn your search into a buy in a few clicks. This makes for a streamlined retail ecosystem. By taking nibbles from every pie, Google has made itself into a fat business empire. For calendar year 2016, they collected $79.38 billion in ad revenue.

So what can browsing Adwords.Google.com do for you? Keywords and key-phrases – which I'll collectively refer to as keywords, except when I don't – are what people search for online. Everybody approaches their searches a little bit differently, however. Some people tend to search products, like my "angora sweater" example. Some think in terms of makers and models, e.g. "Gillette Fusion." Still other people are likely to search for what they want to do with a product—"shaving" instead of "razors." If you build your ads around the wrong keyword, you can cripple your PPC campaign. AdWords has a keyword search tool to help you avoid that pitfall. When you're researching what your customers love, it can help you drill down from general to specific.

A search on "hipsters" in AdWords' Keyword Planner offers a long list of phrases such as "hipster style", "hipster words", and "hipster websites". Ordering by "Avg. monthly searches" reveals something unexpected:

Keyword (by relevance)	Avg. monthly searches ↓ ?	Competition ?	Suggested bid ?	Ad impr. share ?	Add to plan
lingerie	1M – 10M	Medium	$0.78	–	»
bh	100K – 1M	Low	$1.13	–	»
underwear	100K – 1M	Medium	$0.67	–	»
hipster girl	10K – 100K	Low	$3.05	–	»
hipster haircut	10K – 100K	Low	$0.30	–	»

Well, perhaps unexpected is too strong a term. Do these keywords give us any insight into what hipsters like? You bet they do. They also suggests that if we target hipsters in our advertising, we have a good chance of crossing over into broader markets, since the graph of hipsters, people who wear lingerie, and people who like to look at hipsters in lingerie probably weighs heavy on the "like to look" side. That second keyword, "bh", by the way, has a number of possible meanings, ranging from the abbreviation for Bahrain to a Western European term for a bra.

Here's another enlightening example. Searching for "razors", again ordered by monthly search volume, yields the following results.

Keyword (by relevance)	Avg. monthly searches [?] ↓	Competition [?]	Suggested bid [?]	Ad impr. share [?]	Add to plan
razer	100K – 1M	Low	$0.13	–	»
razer blade	100K – 1M	Medium	$0.70	–	»
shaving brush	10K – 100K	High	$0.78	–	»
safety razor	10K – 100K	High	$0.80	–	»
shaving kit	10K – 100K	High	$0.97	–	»
razors for women	10K – 100K	High	$3.06	–	»

The first revelation here is that "razor" is misspelled as often as not, but the most interesting entries I see on this list are "shaving brush" and "razors for women". Enough people are searching these key-phrases that advertisers are in heated competition. While "shaving brush" is relatively cheap, CPC on "razors for women" is through the roof. Am I in a position to buy my way to the top of these searches? Even if not, if I'm serious about making it in the razor business, I'm definitely going to look in to meeting the needs that customers are expressing. Shaving brushes are a must-have as an add-on, and serving women in this market looks to be just as important as serving men.

You can learn a lot by the rise and fall keywords. That's why I keep AdWords open on my desktop all the time. Another great resource I check almost as often is Follow.net. I look to them to track the competition's top keywords, keyword volume, and average CPC. Follow.net will give you an expanded view of where a given site is getting their traffic. Are people coming in from searches, directly typing URLs into their browser's address bar, or clicking links on social media, email, or text and banner ads? Follow.net can show you all this and more. They make a good deal of data available for free, but you'll get access to enhanced options if you set up a payment plan.

The graphs on Follow.net are formatted for quick reading. At a glance, you can get a good feel for ads that worked for your competitor and ads that didn't. Since companies are always bidding on keywords and paying premiums to grab the high spots in searches, seeing the return they get on their investment is a key insight that can save you time and money.

The Role of Innovation

When it comes to giving customers what they want, there is a distinction worth making is between what you can do strictly as a marketer and what you could do as owner or CEO of a company. If your position doesn't allow you control of R&D, there's a limit as to how much you can mold the product line. Being able to decide what gets made is an awesome responsibility, but it's also a huge advantage for a marketer. Even if you're in a situation where your boss drops a core product on your desk on Monday and tells you to sell it, though, you should absolutely think in terms of suggesting add-ons, packages, and features. Connecting production to customer needs and wants is your job, after all.

At Hound Dog Digital Marketing, I've been brought into situations where a company is great at what they do but don't understand how to reach customers. Usually my instructions don't require a major retool of their product line. A nudge here, a push there; like twisting a knob on a pair of binoculars, these adjustments give the company focus. The most important question a company should ask everyday is, "Are we doing what our customers will love?" If the answer is no, marketers are the ones who have to advocate for change.

Now, there is some pushback on this whole "do what they love" thing. The argument goes that if a company is always chasing customer expectations, they'll never have time to innovate. "Look at Apple," people say. "Apple doesn't wait for customers to tell them what to do. They build great stuff and customers buy it, no prior knowledge required." While I agree that innovation is important, the notion that Apple and companies like them don't look to their customers for direction is dead wrong. Apple has made some great intuitive leaps in the past, but they've been able to do so precisely because they pay attention to customer buying habits. In other words, they find out what customers love. The fact of their success is enough to convince me I'm right in my analysis, but I can prove it to skeptics by taking a quick field trip into history.

Steve Jobs famously said, "People don't know what they want until you show it to them" (BusinessWeek, May 25, 1998). The date of that article is interesting. This was fresh off a keynote speech Jobs gave back when he was re-upping as interim Apple CEO on a daily basis. The big customer product Jobs was hyping at the time was the first-generation iMac, an all-in-one PC that looked like it came out of a Jell-O mold. To judge from the sales figures, college kids love Jell-O. Reading Jobs's quote now, it's tempting to think the takeaway is that there's no point paying attention to buying habits, that you've got to lead from way out in front, shouting at slow-poke customers to keep up.

In context, Jobs's position was a lot more nuanced. Responding to interviewer Andy Reinhardt's question about how much customer research went into the iMac, Jobs noted that Apple had a large customer base and was aware of industry trends. "But in the end," Jobs said, "for something this complicated, it's really hard to design products by focus groups." I've got to take a moment to laugh at that. From the perspective of the 1990s, Jobs was a guy who looked like he didn't care about marketing at all, but what he was actually pointing out were the uselessness of models from the data-poor age. Jobs saw beyond focus groups and a keepin'-up-with-the-Joneses approach to product design, devising fresh solutions to customer problems.

It took chutzpah to go against conventional wisdom like that. Back in in 1998, the Internet was all "You've got mail!" and dancing babies. Amazon, founded in 1994, had just begun accumulating their massive database of buying behaviors, and Google was still in twinkle in Larry Page's and Sergey Brin's eyes. From the perspective of today, we know that Steve Jobs won the fight that was just warming up in '98, bringing Apple back to prominence as a world-class technology provider. At the time, what he was talking about was a bold take on customer relations. If you dig into it, his approach comes down to selling solutions. Under Jobs' guidance, Apple ignored focus groups, looked at who their customers were and what they loved. They used that knowledge to come up with new ways to meet their needs. By satisfying the customers they already had, they drew in new customers whose needs weren't being talked about at other companies.

Consider the iPod. People talk about Job's 2001 reveal of the iPod as a transformative event, and it was. But it's not like no one in 2001 had ever thought of carrying their music around in a box clipped to their belt. Sony came out with the Walkman in 1979. So how was it that after decades of people being able to listen to music on the go, Apple saw room for innovation?

Size was the deciding factor. The bulkiness of the medium had always dictated the form factor of Walkmans, and the Discmans that never fully replaced them. So in the late '90s, Sony and others dipped their toes into the digital audio market, producing tiny players that could retrieve music from flash memory. The problem with these devices was that there was no streamlined end-to-end solution for ripping tracks off CDs and getting them loaded for portable use. At least, there wasn't a solution that had been successfully marketed to the public. This was the challenge Apple rose to meet in the early 2000s. They packaged an intuitive interface with a sleek piece of tech and voila! The iPod was born. Without inventing anything completely new, Apple had managed to deliver the first iconic product of the millennium. And Steve Jobs solution sales pitch was classic. "1,000 songs in your pocket". Soon every portable digital music player was being called an "iPod" no matter whose brand was on the package.

Or course, we can't talk about the rise of Apple without mentioning the iPhone, probably the best example of a product being developed in anticipation of customer interest. Cell phones were popular, portable music players were all over the place, and the PDA market was booming by the time the first-generation iPhone debuted. The last thing anybody thought they needed in January 2007 was a combination of these devices. Nobody sat in a focus group and said, "I like my phone, but I wish it played music and had a touch screen and could organize my life." Like the old candy bar commercial about getting your chocolate in my peanut butter, Apple saw that the whole could be more than the sum of its parts. They innovated a surprising device that, all of a sudden, everybody had to have. Did the inspiration for that device come out of the blue? Of course not. Apple followed trends closely, combining creative thinking with deep knowledge of customer interests to spark a revolution whose time had come.

Case Study – Apple vs. Blackberry

In 2010, Apple followed up the iPhone with the iPad. That's when something interesting happened on the competitive side of the technology market. As smart as Apple had been with its previous products, their competitors had never had serious trouble following their lead. One of the most popular contenders for Apple's crown was Research In Motion Limited (RIM), a Canadian company best known for creating the BlackBerry. Thanks to rabid fans who would rather have lost an eyeball than have to text without BlackBerry's physical keypad, RIM had a good thing going. Even the US President was a die-hard user. The company built up an image as a lifestyle provider.

RIM were mavericks who could do anything the other guys could do, only different and better. You didn't need Apple or anybody else if you were on the BlackBerry train.

Raw grit helped the company stay relevant through the dawn of the iPhone era. They held a 20% share in the mobile phone market in 2010 and hit a peak revenue of $19.9 billion the next year. Then along came the PlayBook, RIM's answer to the iPad. In speccing out the PlayBook, RIM showed that you can take being a maverick too far. Instead of slapping a coat of Blackberry paint on an iPad, they stripped their follow-up design of some basic functionality, essentially saying to customers, "You've already got email on your computer. You've already got an organizer on your phone. You don't need an integrated device." In October 2010, six months after the iPad went on sale, they showed off the PlayBook, a tablet without native email or calendar. Citing security concerns, RIM said that users would have to link up to the company's servers through their phones in order to access these communication features. PlayBooks could then be synced with phones via an app, essentially turning the tablet into a $500–$700 monitor.

You don't need 20-20 hindsight to realize this was a stupid idea. After the PlayBook flopped hard, it wasn't long before increased competition in the tech field knocked RIM off its pedestal. The former fan-favorite company bled market share and revenue over the next five years. In 2016, the company doing business as BlackBerry Limited took in just over $2 billion. That's a $17.9 billion downturn compared to their peak and barely a drop in the bucket compared to the $428.9 billion mobile phone market worldwide. In contrast, Apple reported a $208 billion revenue in 2016 and finished the year neck-and-neck with their current competitor for smart phone dominance, Samsung.

It's not hard to see what Apple did right and BlackBerry did wrong. Under Steve Jobs, Apple cared enough to read their customers. They paid attention to features that kept people coming back. They looked for problems and innovated solutions. And they never forgot that customers buy what they love, if a company is smart enough to sell it to them. Thanks to their customer focus, Apple has continued to lead in a crowded field.

RIM had been an early innovator in that same field, but right around the time Apple and their other competitors started turning up the heat, they lost focus. The PlayBook solved nobody's problems and met no customer need. RIM rushed it to market in the name of competition, delivering a sub-par device that ended up looking an also-ran. They compounded their mistake by leaving out features customers already loved in similar devices. The whole process of syncing up a phone just to use basic functionality was a giant step backwards. Did RIM really expect people to reward them for making their lives harder?

Picture yourself sitting down in the meeting that hatched the PlayBook. You can easily imagine somebody ticking off items on a clipboard, saying, "Price? Check. Product? Check. Promotion? Check. Place? Check." Do you think RIM used focus groups? If they got together a room full of dedicated BlackBerry users and asked them, "Would you guys mind syncing your phones with a tablet in order to access email?" I'm betting the answer was, "Sure! Of course. Is there cake later?" Not having been a fly on the wall, I can't say for sure what happened, but it's clear that nobody at RIM took the time to seriously question what the company was doing. Or if they did, they tried to get at the answer from the wrong angle. The question they should have asked and didn't was, "Is this something our customer will love?"

Companies make blunders like the one that sank RIM surprisingly often. They stumble through product launches like a nearsighted tackle trying to blitz the QB. Such unfocused, reactive efforts are all but guaranteed to fail. To avoid this common pitfall, you've got to put the customer's loves first. Instead of reacting, look ahead. Anticipate customer wants and needs. Take time to THINK, even if thinking puts production back a day or two. Brainstorming you next great idea is never going to delay a project half so long as manufacturing and logistical concerns. If you act too fast, you risk getting caught offside. In business, as in football, the winning team isn't necessarily the first inside the end zone. It's the one that paces itself, makes the right plays, and still has something in the tank when the fourth quarter comes around.

3 – Sell Them Solutions

Marketing is a form of communication. It communicates benefits and solutions. The customer has a problem. Your company has a product with a benefit that solves that problem. To translate your solution into sales, you need to convey the benefit to the customer. Doing so effectively requires that you THINK about who your customers is and what they love. Nowadays, finding out how customers spend their time online is easy. But having the data in front of you isn't enough. Solving customer problems requires creativity and experimentation. Selling solutions does too.

Back when I worked with HSN, I got to know Bob Circosta, their Billion Dollar Man. Bob is a gadget guy, always with a new product to sell. Bob's marketing approach for these products is simple and effective. It all comes down to a visual, something you can show on TV. For instance, one day Bob told me about a fabric treatment that blocks stains from setting in. This threw me, because I couldn't see how he was going to pitch a product that literally prevents a visual from happening. You can show a stain, sure. But how do you show a stain's absence? Bob explained his brilliant plan. Later I got to see it in action. Cue flashback.

Bob with his gleaming smile shows a spray bottle containing the product. Next to him is a pedestal holding two swatches of white carpet. There's an overhead camera that the director switches in to give the audience a quick look at both carpets, shiny clean. Then from behind the pedestal, Bob produces a glass of red wine. After apologizing to his co-host for working her nerves—he knows what a clean freak she is, ha ha—he pours out half the glass on one of the carpets. Just soaks it. Of course the swatch is ruined. The co-host cringes, talking about how awful it would be if that was her carpet at home. But wait, Bob tells the audience. Wait until you see what happens with a few sprays of this miracle product.

He applies the spray to the pristine swatch and spills the second glass. Instead of ruining the swatch, the wine beads up like rain on a windshield. Bob lets it sit for a while as he talks through what just happened. Not the technical details, mind, just the fact that this stuff, this stuff right here in this bottle, saved the carpet, saved the hostess's nerves and the imaginary dinner party she was putting on for her friends, maybe saved all the future dinner parties she wouldn't have been able to host due to her soiled reputation. Then Bob sops up the wine with a paper towel. It wipes away clean, leaving behind nothing but a memory. And Bob delivers the catch phrase: "It stops the stain before it starts."

For that product in that market, Bob's perfectly staged presentation was all he needed to engage with his customers. Thinking about the customers who tune into HSN helped Bob devise a way to share the benefits of his miraculous solution. Now, Bob is the best there is at what he does. Pitching gadgets on a dedicated TV network is great work if you can get it, but it is a narrow focus, a niche in the marketing game. The products you're going to launch in your career will almost certainly require a more diverse approach. If you want to enter a crowded marketplace, disruption will be key. Those who don't stand out in the crowd quickly fade away.

What if standing out is not an option? Not long ago I had a client with exactly that problem. He'd invented a process for treating guitar strings that extends their from days or weeks to months. Serious guitar players, guys who go through strings like martini bars go through olives, were going to love this brilliant product. It was unique. Prior to his innovation, the only was to extend the life of a string was to coat it with a chemical similar to Teflon. Dirt from a player's hands or from the environment gets in between the windings of a string and dulls the sound, so plenty of people were excited about coated strings when they came out in the '90s. The problem is that the coating itself makes the strings sound muffled. Musicians listening for that nice, crisp sound, with just a little twang, could tell the difference. Some avoid the coated strings even though replacing the uncoated strings was ultimately more expensive.

The clear leaders in the guitar string industry are Ernie Ball, D'Addario, Elixir. Elixir came out with a coated string some years ago and cornered the market, with no competition at the time. My client's process looked like it could be an even bigger success, since it eliminated the muffling factor. The problem was that the market for guitar strings was too big for him. It's worth around $200 million a year when you factor in acoustic, electric, and bass guitar strings. Complicating matters, the primary distribution channel for strings is retail stores, most of which charge some kind of slotting fee, in addition to warehousing, rebates, discounts accruals and other expenditures, like the supermarkets we discussed earlier. Retailers also tend to be risk averse when it comes to taking in new products, especially unproven ones, since they have to pay upfront for inventory.

My client had seen how hard it was going to be to get his strings in stores, so he decided to try selling them online. He'd invested all his startup money in developing the technology and building the equipment for his process, so paying all those fees wasn't really an option for him. His website was functional, but it didn't click with customers. When he told me his story, I wasn't surprised. It's a common misconception that you can spin up a website and all of a sudden get traffic. Sorry, folks. Even on the Internet, you can't market for free. Unless you happen to already have the expertise I've been highlighting in this book, plus content writing skills and time to manage social media, email campaigns, SEO, etc., it's best to hire out.

I sat down with my client. Taking a realistic look at the numbers, I told him that he'd have to spend another $500,000 to make a dent online. That wasn't pocket change to this guy. It isn't to most people. And I wasn't trying to scare him off. The number reflected how hard it would have been to make a big noise in a competitive field. My client didn't have the money, and his chances of getting it as venture capital were slim. The market simply wasn't big enough to attract serious investment, not with so many incumbents already doing business. Couple the marketing expense the need to build new distribution channels, I said, and the prospects of disrupting the guitar string industry as an independent just didn't look good.

"If you don't have the money," I said, "the best thing we can do is get some sales on Amazon. I can do that efficiently, with little cash outlay." Then, if we got enough interest, the customers would start making the noise we needed. Major competitors would take notice, and one of them might get nervous enough to make an offer. They already had the infrastructure in place, after all, so were in a far better position to get the most out of his invention. "If you have a couple hundred thousand dollars invested in this and they buy you for a million, or a million-and-a-half, which they will do if they see a viable opportunity to take a competitor out of the market, it's worth it."

Agreeing with me that this was the best end scenario to shoot for, we shook hands. Soon we were able to make those initial sales on Amazon. Customers gave the product good reviews and we took advantage of some co-branding opportunities with top names in audio and guitars. I was able to get my client's product showing in the top 10 search results on Amazon for several key categories – "electric guitar strings" and "acoustic guitar strings" among others. This brought more people in to see the brand and post their reviews. Getting in the decision set was critical. If people can't see you, you're not going to sell. Our ranking didn't just happen, it took months of giving deep discounts to affiliate sites, building our presence on social media, and running ads. Once we did break in, things happened fast. We started to trend, which boosted our visibility with top competitors.

My client had several meaningful conversations with major companies before deciding to cut a deal. He sold the business at a fair price and was able to continue shepherding his process as a consultant for the buyer. Was it the outcome he envisioned? No. Was it the best we could hope for under the circumstances? Considering our financial constraints, I believe it was. My client's process offered the best solution for a discriminating subset of guitar players. Making a loud enough sound to attract our customers was a challenge best suited to a company who could crank the volume to eleven. Everybody benefited – client, company, customers, and me. The solution to selling our solution was a win-win.

The Power of Content Marketing

Academic types have a thing for definitions. I understand why. It's hard to get into a topic without framing it first. It's like building a house. You have to anchor the studs before you can put up drywall. When it comes to marketing, what gets me is how so many definitions miss out on the idea of selling the customer a solution. It's not like this concept is new. Content marketing has been around since the 1890s. Companies around that time started to create ads that told problem-solution stories about their brands. This was the heyday of newspapers, when businesses in major cities used to advertise everything from cigarettes to dental appliances, ladies' corsets to farm equipment. Early print marketers went out of their way to try and connect with their customers, even though they lived in an age when finding out what they loved meant a lot of guess work and house-to-house visits.

The introduction of radio marked the beginning of broadcast marketing. Spend a couple minutes listening to some old-time radio ads on YouTube and you'll hear plenty of examples of selling solutions. Old TV ads start to show a downward trend. You'll see fewer attempts to ENGAGE in the black-and-white TV era, when celebrity endorsements were king. The best TV ads, then and now, show products people love being enjoyed by actors who look like the images customers have of themselves. How many luxury car owners spend their weekends zipping along a high mountain pass? Not as many as ads would have us believe. Car companies recycle that image because there's something about being above it all that makes committing a good chunk of your paycheck to a care lease feel worthwhile.

From '89 to '95 I was a senior exec at Sutton Place Gourmet, a prestigious specialty food brand that stood for quality and unique food items from around the world. We stocked hard-to-find cheeses, wines, meats, and groceries. We made our own ice cream and roasted our own coffee long before Starbucks went nationwide. We employed French chefs, pastry chefs, and bakers, all creating unique desserts. Price was never an issue. Our customers didn't care about price. Shopping in our stores was like driving a Mercedes or a Jaguar. A reputation for luxury brought customers through the door. Once they saw what we had to offer, they were happy to pay anything we asked.

The shopping bags we sent home with folks were more than just for toting goods. They were made of high-quality paper, with rope handles. They had our logo printed on the side. Though the bag cost us a little more to make, it became one of our best promotional vehicles. The Washington Post once showed an image of a Sutton Place bag sitting on the curb alongside other exotic throwaways in an article about wealth in the marketplace. Customers used to mail us photos of the bag in famous locales. You didn't think Facebook was the first place people shared their vacation pics, did you? We had great shots of the bag on top of the Eiffel Tower, against the sandy backdrop of a Middle Eastern desert, and sitting on the Great Wall of China. These and other photos were blown up to poster size and hung in stores. The bag became symbolic of our customers, who they were, what they loved. It was a badge of honor to be able to shop in our stores. Our customers wanted the finest food money could buy. We provided their solution and they displayed our bags with pride.

Many of our most popular products were imported. In some cases, what made them special was obvious. Other items required explanation. The monthly newsletter that went out to our customers did much of the heavy lifting. The woman who wrote it was fantastic at weaving a compelling story. One time we imported an exclusive, high-quality olive oil. The pedigree and the price were both beyond first cold-pressed extra virgin. We're talking ambrosia of the gods, with a retail price around $50 per liter. This product did solve a problem for the customer – "What'll I drizzle over my salmon mince bruschetta?" – but communicating that solution was a challenge.

The newsletter told a tale of our buyer walking through Tuscany and stumbling on an out-of-the-way olive orchard. After some convincing, the owner conducts her on a cellar tour. His special oil is kept separate from the rest of the harvest, he explains. Most customers are used to cheap imitations, so they cannot appreciate premium grade. But the bella signora? She has the eye, or the nose, or whatever it takes to tell great oil from good. She talks him into exporting a small amount of his stock and one ocean crossing later, it appears on store shelves. The exclusivity of the premium oil, brought home by this narrative, helped Sutton Place sell out of that small batch in two weeks. The company was happy with the sales, and customers were thrilled to be able to show their friends what real olive oil is like. That's the power of content marketing.

It doesn't take a miracle to sell a $50 bottle of olive oil. All it takes is communicating its benefits as a solution. Not all solutions are equal. Some require more explanation than others. Problems, on the other hand, are universal.

The Ultimate Shave

Some years ago, I was on a business trip way out of town. As sometimes happens, I found that I'd left a crucial piece of gear at home, my razor. I went to a store thinking this was no big deal, that I could pick up a spare and be on my way. But the prices the stores wanted to charge quickly made me see red. $36 for a pack of Gillette's at the time? What a rip-off! As I paid this exorbitant sum, I realized I couldn't be the only guy in the country fuming over the cost of a smooth chin. It was then that I decided to disrupt the shaving industry. I'd do my research, find the bottleneck in the delivery system, and engineer a solution that customers like me would love.

The first question I decided to look into was, "Why do eight Gillette razors cost $36, while supermarkets sell their store brand at eight for $9.99?" I figured there must be a difference in quality, but in fact the reason has little to do with the product itself. It's a reflection of the supermarket shortsightedness I talked about in Chapter 1. Razors are one of a number of products that stores deliberately low ball, reasoning that all customers care about is price. Which is stupid. In my experience as a shopper, one look at the price discrepancy was enough to scare me off the store brand. I wanted a good shave, not a slit throat! If the stores were smart, they'd price their razors at $19.99. That's enough of discount to grab a customer's attention, but not so massive that it looks like the store is trying to pass off second-rate goods.

The reality is, most store brand razors are on a par with name brands. A huge percentage of them are manufactured by a company called Personna, owned by Energizer, the corporation that also owns Schick. Before their acquisition,

Personna was one of the oldest razor manufacturers in the world. They got started around the same time as Gillette, in Brooklyn, NY, 1875. Depending how old you are, you might even remember seeing Personna commercials on TV in the '50s and '60s. Back then, it was a trusted brand. That trust fell by the wayside in the '80s when Personna got bought out by a couple of venture capital groups, whose snatch and grab mentality drove the company out of the market.

Lacking a strong name but still having solid infrastructure, Personna reinvented itself as the largest private label manufacturer of razors and razor blades. Thanks to their purchase by Energizer, they now have access to Schick technology. Think about that for a second. A private label manufacturer owned by Schick's parent company, with a century-plus of history and know-how. Sounds like a pretty safe investment of your shaving dollars, right? Yet retailers who sell Personna products under their store brands price them for peanuts. Personna cartridges sell for $5 a four pack in stores that sell Schick at $16 for four. Crazy, huh? Examples like this are yet more evidence that supermarkets don't care about solving customer problems. Without doing the research, how is the average customers supposed to know they're getting a good deal on a pack of store brand razors? It's sheer ignorance and industrial momentum that keeps supermarkets in the "price is value" mentality.

Now that I knew it was possible to produce quality razors at a decent price, I was ready to pioneer new channels to distribute those razors. I co-founded a company, 800Razors. com, to sell shaving equipment and accessories online. Monthly subscriptions boxes had been popularized by Birchbox not long before, and though they were only part of our business, I saw their potential as a tool to get customers hooked on our products. Unfortunately, it took longer than I would have liked to work out the logistics and secure investment and ideas, like sniffles, are contagious, so by the time we launched, we already had competitors making waves in the industry. For 800Razors.com to become viable, I was going to have to make some big noise on social media.

At the time, LA Dodgers pitcher Brian Wilson was one of the biggest names in baseball. Fans liked his fastball, but most tuned in to marvel at his epic beard. He'd been growing it out for three years when I got the idea to offer him $1 million to shave it clean with one of my razors. The idea of getting razor blades by mail was still new. People wondered about the quality of our razors, and more to the point, the quality of our shave. I had anticipated this going in, so while price and convenience set us apart from the supermarkets, what we were selling was The Best Shave At The Best Price, Guaranteed. 800Razors.com was the website. The Ultimate Shave™ was the brand. How better to get people talking about that brand than by shaving off a famous beard?

People have since asked me if I was serious, if the company really would have paid the million bucks. The answer is, absolutely. The interest we got on social media and in the blogosphere was worth seven figures. Just making the offer brought a major bump in traffic and conversions. Imagine what a clean-shaven Brian Wilson raving about our products would have done! Though he enthusiastically refused, the publicity we got on both ends of the stunt propelled our new company to a couple hundred-thousand monthly subscribers. This shows that having a quality product isn't enough. You've got to get your product on customer radar. There are tons of ways to do that, but these days, it's hard to beat a social media storm.

It's also hard to make lightning strike twice. After the Brian Wilson furor died down, I knew I had to do something to keep the ball rolling. This was critical because we were, in terms of THINK-ENGAGE-THRIVE, at the end of one cycle and the start of another. We'd identified our customers, designed initial offerings, and built infrastructure: THINK. We'd found something our customers loved and connected through it to sell a solution: ENGAGE. The sign-ups and sales we got from thinking and engaging pushed us into THRIVE. My marketing drive had been successful, but I wasn't close to done. Now that we were thriving, it was time to grow the business.

There are multiple methods of reinvesting. One is to start with a core product line, build out, then replace underperforming players. Another is to set a fixed number of SKUs. Costco does brilliantly at this. Every category at Costco is allowed just 15 SKUs. If a product manager is shopping around for new vendors or the next hot product from an existing vendor, they knows they have a decision to make. Before a new item can come in, something old has to go. This differs from the first method because the managers aren't cutting away dead wood, they're grafting in a new branch. Maybe there's not a SKU that stands out as a loser. It's tempting to leave a moderately performing product line alone. But you can't move forward standing still. A good product manager will look at sales and ask, "Do customers really love this product anymore?" Flat sales, or growth so slow that other SKUs in the same category blow it away, are indications it's time for a change.

With 800Razors.com, we started out selling high-quality, American made razors for men and women. A natural evolution was to come up with shave creams, one for men and one for women. These had different scents and did slightly different things. The key benefit we decided to promote was moisturizing. Our creams didn't just lubricate, they put moisture into the skin, improving the texture and bringing hairs to shave to the surface. Not only did this mean a closer shave, it gave skin a silky feel. After the creams debuted, we got comments from customers that their significant other had touched their skin and been surprised by its smoothness. Sales grew and subscriptions went up.

With that victory in the bag, THINK-ENGAGE-THRIVE cycled back around. My team thought about how to follow up. Since customers liked what we'd done to the beginning and middle of the shaving experience, the next logical offering was some sort of aftershave. This solved a problem especially for our women customers. In winter time, everybody's skin gets dry. Shaving a yard of leg is a hassle anyway. What's the point, if the air is going to make those legs dry and itchy? Our solution to this age-old problem was a line of moisturizing aftershaves that turned out to be a real game changer for women who'd been grudgingly giving up on shaving during low-humidity months.

The moisturizes we used weren't oily or greasy. They absorbed into the skin instead of gooping on the surface. Customers loved 'em. They started sending us videos. One showed a dude shaving in his bathroom mirror. He was using a shave brush and shave soap, rather than one of our cream products, but he was using our razor. It was fascinating to watch him work through his routine. He would wet the soap puck by adding water to the mug that held it, whip the water and soap with the brush into a frothy emulsion, then slather foam on his face. I found this particularly interesting because I'd always figured that the guys who went to so much trouble were also using straight razors and a strop, neither or which really fit our line. But I did a little research, talked to several serious shavers, and come to find out, there are lots of men who enjoy the ritual of adding puck to mug and brushing on the soap, but who feel the same way I do about the convenience and safety of a modern razor.

The team decided to go big or go home. Soon we were selling kits with a mug, puck, and brush, all branded with our logo. Not only were these a fantastic gift item for the holidays, we also quickly got comments that customers loved the soap. They'd buy four or five pucks at a time, which worked great for us, since the kits were usually a one-time purchase. You only need one soap mug, after all, and a good brush can get you through a year, but the soap – all-natural, like our cream and aftershave – was an indulgence they enjoyed using up. When I'd first suggested selling the kits, the rest of the team had laughed. They'd thought it was a cute idea, but that it'd never be more than a niche item. I pulled rank, got the kits made, and soap pucks turned out to be one of our best sellers. I've still got a kit myself. Not only does soaping up provide a better shave, there really is something about the ritual that I can't quite describe. You have to try it for yourself to understand.

No matter what form your reinvestment takes, the key is being constantly on the lookout for new ways to serve your customers. In the shaving business, this meant understanding how people approach the problem of a daily/semi-weekly/ whatever shave. Women have different needs than men, so serving them meant different products with a different approach. Some men are just about minimizing the bite of time shaving takes out of their day, while others invest in multiple products for different days of the week. If they're pushed for time, these super shavers will shave in the shower using their Gillette, but on the weekends, they break out the brush, the puck, maybe even a straight razor. By selling a diverse array of products, we were able to maximize retention and increase customer loyalty. Incidentally, this approach mirrored that of Steve Jobs. We looked at behavior, saw how customers did things, and were able to project what trends were going to take off.

One more story about 800Razor.com before we move on. This one's a cautionary tale. I don't regret my actions, but the events did confirm a belief I've long held about celebrity endorsements. They can be great in the short term, but they can also go wrong for a company. After the Brian Wilson stunt, I didn't wait for another major leaguer to make his facial hair famous. The company was headquartered in Baltimore, Maryland, a great town that also happens to be home to Olympic legend Michael Phelps. When I looked at Michael's profile, both on- and offline, I thought, "This guy is an influencer." The idea of paying somebody to brag about my product doesn't appeal to me, and I didn't have the budget to offer Michael the kind of money he was attracting at the time, but the congruity of a swimmer saying kind words about my razors and creams was too good to pass up.

In my own athletic past, I used to compete in triathlons. I can tell you that there's nothing quite like the feeling of jumping into a cold pool after shaving your whole body. It's a shock to the system, and anybody who has to deal with it on a regular basis would want to mitigate the sensation any way they can. The moisturizing effect of our shave cream, designed by veterans of the beauty industry, was a godsend to these customers. So when Michael was getting ready for the 2016 Olympics, I decided to drop off a razor and shave cream care package at the Meadowbrook Aquatic Center, where he'd been training for years. If nothing else, I thought, he might mention the gift in a couple Instagram posts to his eight-million plus subscribers.

Two weeks later, I got an email. Michael said he liked the razors and the cream. He was close to running out, so could drop off more samples? I was happy to oblige. If he happened to throw out a post about us, that'd be nice, I said. I didn't get pushy. I didn't have to. Our product was a solution he couldn't find anywhere else. Not long after I dished out Michael's seconds, he emailed to ask for thirds, because his girlfriend had stolen what he had left. I offered to drop off some women's razors with the next care package and happily followed through.

A few days later, I got a call from Michael's manager. He summed up events, mentioned that Michael liked the products, that he'd posted about us on Instagram, and asked if there was an opportunity for us to work together. I was up front, telling him that I wasn't looking to do an endorsement deal. If Michael wanted to invest, however, I'd be glad to work out the equity. The fact that he liked both the razors and the add-ons made this an easy call for Michael. We reached an arrangement whereby he'd take a bigger share of profits if he put out commercials and social media promotions. This made financial sense for him. On my side, it couldn't have looked better. If things went smoothly, an audience of millions would be thinking about 800Razors.com every time Michael showed his bare chest. If you watched the Rio Olympics, you know that was often.

The sports press picked up the story of Michael's investment. He did his part on social media, and soon we saw another bump in subscriptions as his followers trafficked our site. Then a strange thing happened. Some of our social media noise turned negative. People brought up the photo of Michael smoking pot at a party back in 2009. Never mind that he's the most decorated Olympian in history, right? They were ready to trash the guy who went on to finish his Olympic career having brought home a total of 23 gold medals for America. It made no sense to me, but that's how things go. I was glad I hadn't signed him to an endorsement deal, because if I had, I would have felt I hadn't gotten my money's worth. This was through no fault of Michael's. He gave the push his all. Celebrity is a funny business.

By the time negativity reached a fever pitch, competition from online shaving clubs had gotten pretty stiff. I decided to sell 800Razors.com to one such club. It wasn't how I'd hoped things would work out, but I signed the papers without regrets. Thinking about guys like me sick who were sick of being gouged for brand name razors had pointed me in the direction of a solution that worked. The Brian Wilson campaign, the expansion of our product line, and even the puritanical bashing of Michael Phelps had all been educational experiences. I'd made some money and walked away with an enhanced my personal brand, my name forever associated with disruptive, organic marketing in the digital age.

Useful Tools: Alexa by Amazon

Very few companies get the chance to blaze a trail into virgin territory. The rest of us have to look for ways to disrupt, to improve on what others are doing, to carve out a niche. Knowing what's happening in your space is essential to all these goals, even if your plan winds up being, "do the opposite of everybody else". When I want to know what my competitors are doing, the first place I look is Alexa.com, which is owned and operated by Amazon. As the fastest company ever to reach $100 billion in revenue, Amazon is a good place to go for advice.

Alexa is a subscription service. You can get some information for free, but the good stuff is is behind a pay wall. Don't worry. Once you're in, you won't regret the investment. Alexa will give you feedback on your own websites. They're a good source for improving your SEO and tracking down broken site links. But like I mentioned above, the big selling point for Alexa is access to your competitors' keyword matrix. Alexa lets you see how keywords are working for the other guys. That's valuable information. At Hound Dog Digital Marketing, we bid on thousands of keywords for our clients. Some keywords are a waste of money. They don't trigger site visits, so they don't convert into sales. Knowing what's working for the competition helps us look past the losers to put money where it's going to count.

Alexa's keyword analysis features make it similar to other tools, but this is by no means a bad thing, since having a couple of different sources of keyword information will help weed out any bias that might have crept into a site's software. But Alexa can do more than provide keyword contrast. It's an excellent tool for examining competitors' back links. Where do they get customers coming from? Are they linking bloggers or reviewers online? If so, I need to consider getting my product in front of those reviewers and their colleagues. Exploring the back links a step further can show how the competitor had been attracting news coverage. They'll no doubt link to articles that show the company in a positive light. Check the byline to see who did the write-up. What was it about the competitor's marketing that caught the writer's attention? Sometimes it pays to reach out to those writers, explaining that you've got a product that does the same job, only better thanks to some x-factor.

Paying attention to the back links is smart because Google, Yahoo, and Bing look at these when calculating Quality Score. High QS means that your site is credible, that it has expert status on a given keyword. If I've got two hundred reviewers back-linking my line of hipster negligees, my site will have a higher QS than HipsterCloset.com, which has only ten links.[5] If my competition in a given field is doing something right, I want to cover the same ground, then go broader and deeper. When I want to build a picture of who's doing what in an industry, I start by making a list of the biggest names. Then I research specific metrics about their sites.

Here's an example, looking at what the razor market is like today. Numbers in the following graph indicate global page rank. Sites in the 10,000s are turning up in searches a hundred times more frequently than sites in the millions, and so on.

---

[5]At the time of writing, the domain HipsterCloset.com is for sale.

Historical Traffic Trends: Alexa Traffic Rank

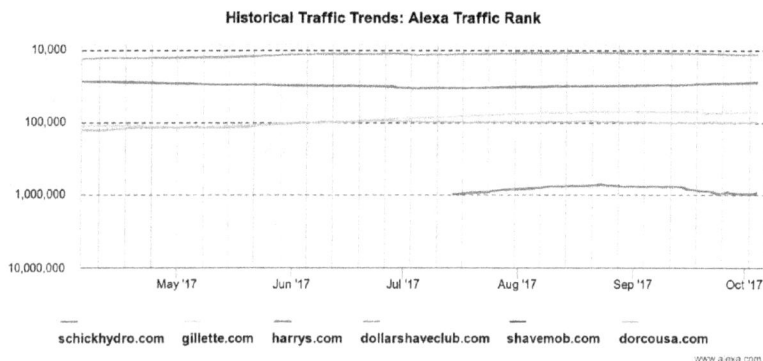

| schickhydro.com | gillette.com | harrys.com | dollarshaveclub.com | shavemob.com | dorcousa.com |

www.alexa.com

This graph shows a solid ranking by Dollarshaveclub.com and Harrys.com, from April to October 2017. There's some interesting tradeoff between Gillette.com and Dorcousa.com in the same period. We see a strong debut by Schickhydro.com in mid-July, when the company started selling subscription plans for blades that fit both Schick and Gillette razors, but you can see the company has a long way to go.

Let's look at what monthly site visits can tell us. The following graph shows average monthly visits over three months.

Monthly Visits

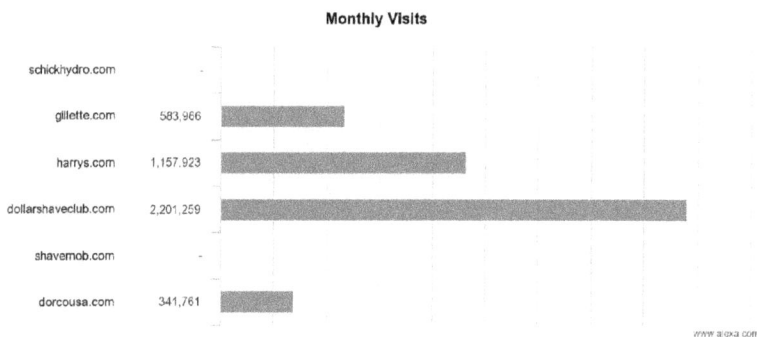

schickhydro.com	
gillette.com	583,966
harrys.com	1,157,923
dollarshaveclub.com	2,201,259
shavemob.com	
dorcousa.com	341,761

www.alexa.com

From this graph, it's clear Dollarshaveclub.com has a solid lead over the competition. They haven't mounted a major campaign I'm aware of, so I put this down mostly to repeat customers. I can test my hypothesis by looking at how engaged the traffic is on their site, compared to everybody else's. A high bounce rate means that people are coming to a site to browse, not buy. Either they're not serious shoppers or the company's not doing enough to hold their interest.

Site ♦	Pageviews/User ♦		Bounce Rate ♦		Time on Site (minutes) ♦	
schickhydro.com	2.00		63.20%		2:42	
gillette.com	2.50	▲ 10.00%	55.40%	▼ 7.00%	2:29	▲ 7.00%
harrys.com	3.26	▼ 5.23%	40.70%	▲ 7.00%	3:10	
dollarshaveclub.com	2.87	▼ 3.04%	47.10%	▲ 6.00%	3:17	▼ 1.00%
shavemob.com	2.90		42.10%		2:56	
dorcousa.com	4.10	▼ 0.24%	33.80%	▲ 1.00%	4:07	▼ 17.00%

Evidence here is not hard to read. The bounce rate for our market leader is in the middle of the pack. The fact that it grew by 6.00% suggests that customers may be losing interest. People are spending less time on Dollarshaveclub. com on average, while Gillette.com has showed significant improvement, despite having a higher bounce rate overall. It seems Gillette has been making noise and they're starting to get results.

Where is all this traffic coming from? Knowing that would clue me in to how my competitors have been attracting customers, if I wanted to get back into the shave game. I'd spend a lot of time looking at this next chart to find out how I could start peeling away competitor traffic.

Traffic Sources

Website	search	social	link	direct
schickhydro.com	15%	25%		55%
gillette.com	34.23%	15.11%		50.1%
harrys.com	15.27%	10.14%		71.4%
dollarshaveclub.com	16.28%			75.12%
shavemob.com	25%			75%
dorcousa.com	19.73%			72.42%

www.alexa.com

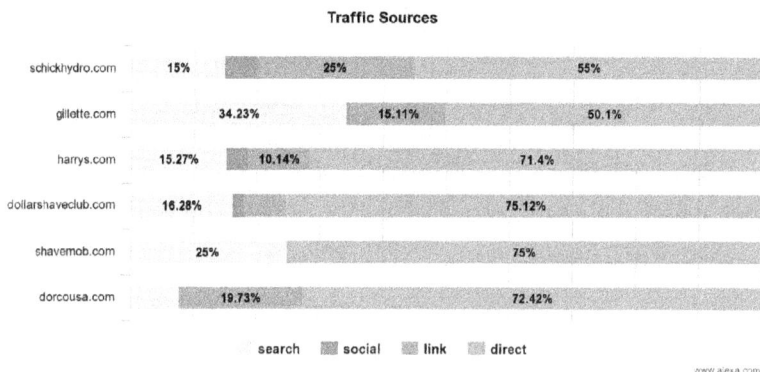

Focus in on Gillette.com. See that 34.23% of their traffic that's coming in through search? Since they're attracting just under 600,000 monthly visits, we can estimate that customers are following search links to Gillette.com about 200,000 times a month. They're making big bids on keywords and keeping their QS high. It'll be worth my while to go deeper into just what they're doing, but I'm going to stick a pin in my analysis for now. We're swamped with numbers, so it's time I talked about how important they are. I'll pick up this example in the next chapter, after introducing some additional tools.

4 – Run the Numbers

If you want to make it in business, it pays to be a data junkie. During my time operating 800Razors.com, I learned that when it comes to being responsive to the data, you can never do too much. I used to look at the website constantly. Real-time feeds showed me how visitors were accessing the site. I checked to see where my customers were coming from, what links they were following, and what sort of devices they were using. The experience was not unlike watching shoppers at a mall through the walls of a glass elevator. I'd watch pack move in together, following the general traffic flow. Then an individual would catch my eye. I'd trace people from one location to another, paying special attention to where they exited. That told me where the site lost their interest. Based on my observations, I oversaw changes to all site pages, particularly checkout, which went through something like twenty-five different versions over the life of the company.

None of those changes were free, but they were worth it. Say it cost me $1000 per week to update the website. Thanks to these changes, I draw in 1000 new visitors per week. The average conversion rate – visitors converting to customers – hovers around three percent across online retailers. There are some terrific sites with conversions in the teens, and Amazon can convert in the low twenties. Numbers like that are out of reach for a startup, so when I was thinking about the changes I pushed for on 800Razors.com, I figured that out of every thousand site visits, we'd convert 1000 times 3% = 30 sales. I asked myself, "What would happen if I boosted conversion to four or five percent?" With no increase in content, I'd be getting forty, fifty sales a week, just by improving site flow. Like a cyclist gearing while pedaling uphill, I'd get superior output from work put in.

Tracing through what helped people convert was eye-opening. Sometimes changing the color or the size of a button made all the difference. Sometimes it was the placement of an image. My team worked like scientists, using A/B testing. We'd change a single element of a page, then watch what happened. Changing more than a single element would have made it impossible to identify the difference maker, so it was important to be methodical. This is the first thing we look at with any client we have. Maximizing site conversions is the best way to grow your sales. You are already spending the ad dollars to drive site visits. Maximize those visits into conversions.

We used Amazon as a lead-generation tool. A lot of eCommerce companies get caught up in the pro-con Amazon debate. There's no question Amazon has grown the online retail pie. Some people resent the size of their slice. But here's the thing. Fifty-two percent of all product searches occur on Amazon today. For comparison's sake, thirty percent occur on Google. However you personally feel about the company, Amazon is where your customers go when they're in the mood to shop. If you're not selling on Amazon, you're missing out. Will Amazon compromise your efforts to drive traffic to your own branded sites? Maybe in the short term. But when you look at product visibility, there's really no contest. If your product is on Amazon, people are going to see it in much higher numbers than if you're only selling on a new, branded site. The smart play is to let Amazon lead customers to you.

Once you've got brand recognition, the fans will follow your brand home.

Every razor on the market is on Amazon, so when we launched 800Razors.com, I knew we needed to have a presence. Since I didn't want Amazon to be the one-stop shop for our brand, I put sets – a handle plus starter supply of blades – on sale. When customers decided they liked our quality and wanted replacement blades, they'd find Amazon didn't offer that option. Some customers emailed asking where they could get replacement blades outside of a kit. Because of Amazon's policies, we couldn't tell them flat out to go to our website, but since our "Sold By" included the site name, most got the message.

Here's the interesting part. Out of every 100 customers who first bought from us via Amazon, more than 70 came over to our site and bought direct from that point on. If that's not enough to calm your fears of Amazon cannibalizing your brand, I don't know what will. Seeding Amazon with product presence, then bringing customers to a branded site, is a strategy I've implemented successfully for myself and quite a few of my clients. Once traffic starts to run your way, your work is cut out for you – check what's working, test to find what's not, update and repeat. Watching the numbers will show you what customers love on a granular level.

Useful Tools: Google Analytics and Experiments

If your company has an eCommerce website, you probably already use Google Analytics, the third in my Holy Trinity of Google. The free data Analytics provides is ridiculously informative. How many people are visiting your site each day? At what times do you hit peak traffic? From where in the world are your visitors connecting? From what part of the country? Are they viewing your pages on a PC, tablet, or mobile phone? Do they browse using Microsoft Edge, Mozilla Firefox, or Google Chrome? There's so much detail, it's hard to know what to do with it all, which is a nice problem to have.

Analytics is great for testing the effectiveness of your ongoing promotions. Did you send out a broadcast email with a unique URL? GA can tell you how many visitors followed that link. What about your Pay Per Click (PPC) ads? Analytics can give you insight into the return on that investment. Incoming links through Google or Yahoo reflect the strength of your site's Search Engine Optimization.

Several of my favorite features are visual tools that allow you to conceptualize data in different ways. My favorite is heat-mapping, which color codes traffic reports to make the peaks pop out. It should go without saying that Google's data sources are top notch. People spend thousands on supplementary programs that do nothing but massage data that Analytics will let you look at for free. I don't fault them for that. Sometimes getting a new angle is worth the investment. Before you can decide if a given tool will work for you, though, you need to what Analytics has to offer.

A plugin that we use at Hound Dog Digital Marketing quite often is Google Analytics Content Experiments. This allows us to A/B test site changes on a percentage of our users. The changes and target percentage are both set in the Analytics web interface. You can also set goals you're looking to accomplish by making the changes in Analytics and get feedback on how you missed, met, or exceeded those goals after the experiment has run for awhile. It's a great way to test a gut feeling or a suggestion made by a small number of users without exposing all your traffic to the change. Seeing side-by-side statistics on your original design and the tweaked version makes it super obvious which one is superior, too.

Useful Tools: iSpionage and SpyFu

When you're ready to craft ads for your campaign, competitors' ads can be a valuable source of inspiration. A great tool for looking at their effectiveness is iSpionage.com. For a fee, the site's proprietary algorithm will analyze ad copy and assign what they call an Ad Effectiveness Index, or AEI. This is based in part on longevity, but also takes into account positioning and other factors conducive to getting eyes-on. You can drill down on iSpionage to look at the traffic an individual ad has generated over its lifespan. I've found it to be a big help in spotting deep trends. Sometimes reviewing historic data sparks creative ideas. If a competitor has been running an ad with an index in the 90s and getting a couple thousand visits per month, it's worth your time to figure out what they've been doing right.

You can dig deeper into keywords with iSpionage, too. Their Keyword Effectiveness Index (KEI) works on a hundred-point scale, with higher numbers indicating keywords with a better track record. It's useful to have a tool like this at your disposal, since a keyword can be a good fit for the product but still fail to drive traffic due to low search volume. That's what we call a long-tail keyword. It's important to weed them out ASAP, as decision to place bids on a keyword should focus on what customers want, not necessarily on what suits the product.

It's vital to get the high-volume keywords nailed down before considering keywords with a volume that runs less than your target per month.

When I say "high volume", think thousands or tens of thousands of searches per month. That's the kind of traffic a retailer needs to grow. A business can't maintain that level of customer interest without fanatical pruning of their keywords. All markets change over time. Keywords that boom one month can go bust the next. When you analyze a competitor's high KEI keyword, pay attention to how long it's been in use. Check it against the trends. Is the keyword going to keep driving conversion in the short term? The data iSpionage provides helps you pick winners, but you've still got to apply common sense and pay attention to the big picture.

Another tool that gives insight on effective keywords is SpyFu. The slant they offer on data is less about finding out what customers are searching now and more about knowing how steep a climb you've got in front of you. Enter a keyword and SpyFu will tell you how much you can expect to spend in the Google auction and how tough it will be to place your site at the top of search engine results for that keyword. For instance, "razors" is currently given a "RANKING DIFFICULTY" of 50, while "Disney" gets a 73. Topping the "razors" search is a tall order, but it's no Space Mountain.

Back on the customer front, SpyFu also lists related keywords the competition is using to link their products. They'll rank a site's SEO and show you how much this optimization helps drive traffic versus how much the competitor is spending on keywords and paid ads. All of these comparisons help me spot weaknesses in the competition's marketing that I can exploit. At the end of the day, if you're launching a new product in a competitive market, your competition is starting out with an advantage. They've been around longer, giving them an edge in terms of experience and brand recognition. Any chisel that can chip away at that advantage is worth taking up.

A Great Shave Revisited

Look back at the example we discussed last chapter, where I used Alexa to find out how the major players are shaping the shaving industry today. Gillette stuck out at me as being worth taking a deeper look into. They're getting a large percentage of their traffic from search results, which I know must be driven by effective keywords. Here's how I'd use iSpionage and Spyfu to do some detailed analysis.

First, I'd check iSpionage, to see what keywords Gillette's on Demand Shave Club is targeting and how their expenditures on PPC and SEO are stacking up against other big names. The following chart shows what they've spent on ads over the last 30 days. It also indicates how many keywords they are targeting with their ads.

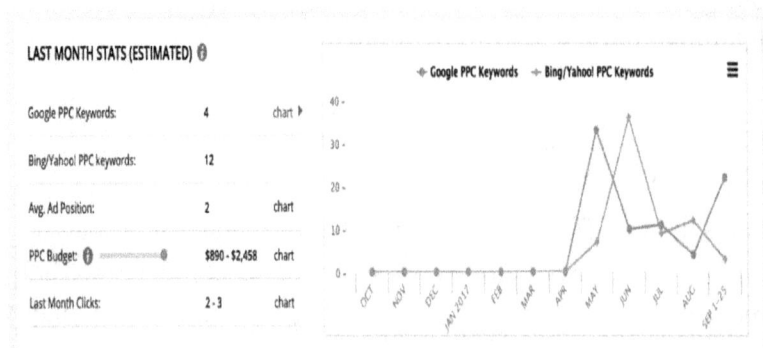

LAST MONTH STATS (ESTIMATED) ⓘ		
Google PPC Keywords:	4	chart ▶
Bing/Yahoo! PPC keywords:	12	
Avg. Ad Position:	2	chart
PPC Budget: ⓘ	$890 - $2,458	chart
Last Month Clicks:	2 - 3	chart

I'm particularly interested in the keywords that have been the most profitable for them. The higher the KEI, shown in the next table's the fifth column, the strong that keyword's performance has been.

	Keyword	Ads	KEI	CPC ($)	Average Search Volume	Average Position	Days Seen	First Seen	Last Seen
☐ ⚙	shaving clubs	3	88.68	3.16	170	2	124	5/23/2017	9/23/2017
☐ ⚙	razor shave club	2	88.34	2.04	70	3	128	5/20/2017	9/24/2017
☐ ⚙	dollar shave club executive review	2	88.08	4.65	320	2	123	5/23/2017	9/22/2017
☐ ⚙	mens shaving club	2	87.98	1.51	170	2	120	5/28/2017	9/24/2017
☐ ⚙	monthly razors	2	87.51	2.44	90	2	114	6/3/2017	9/24/2017
☐ ⚙	dollar shave club discount	2	87.2	6.31	90	2	123	5/23/2017	9/22/2017
☐ ⚙	dollar shave club blade review	3	95.55	1.95	390	2	122	5/21/2017	9/19/2017
☐ ⚙	gillette offers	2	85.2	1.47	10	1	118	5/24/2017	9/18/2017
☐ ⚙	razor a month	2	82.04	1.43	210	3	115	5/27/2017	9/18/2017
☐ ⚙	monthly shave club	3	63.8	2.35	480	2	97	5/18/2017	8/22/2017

This is a great eagle's eye view. Now I want to see the ads attached to the most profitable keywords. Take "shaving clubs", the highest KEI result from above, for example.

	Keyword	Ads	KEI	CPC ($)	Average Search Volume	Average Position	Days Seen	First Seen	Last Seen
☐ ⚙	shaving clubs	3	88.68	3.16	170	2	124	5/23/2017	9/23/2017

Ad Copy	AEI	Destination Url	Other Keywords	Average Position	Days Seen	Last Seen
Gillette Shave Club - Is Now Gillette On Demand - gillette.com ondemand.gillette.com/ Factory Floor to your Door. Value & Convenience. Shop Razors, On Demand.	32.12	https://www.ondemand.gillette.com/	0	1	1	9/23/2017
Gillette Shave Club - Is Now Gillette On Demand - gillette.com ondemand.gillette.com/ Factory Floor to your Door. Best Value & Convenience. Shop Razors, On Demand.	18.14	http://clickserve.dartsearch.net/link/click? id=43700020271960679&ds_s_kwgid=5870000237994...	6	2	1	7/15/2017
Gillette Shave Club - Is Now Gillette On Demand - gillette.com ondemand.gillette.com/ Experience The New Gillette On Demand Today and Receive $3 Off Your First Order	11.95	http://clickserve.dartsearch.net/link/click? id=43700020271960622&ds_s_kwgid=5870000237994...	29	2	1	5/23/2017

Now, that is an interesting contrast. Even though "shaving clubs" is Gillette's most effective keyword, the ads they're attaching are scraping the bottom of the barrel. That 32.12 AEI for the 9/23/17 ad is pitiful! A glance at the ads is all I need to tell you why these aren't working for the company. Nobody cares that "Gillette Shave Club Is Now Gillette On Demand". I mean, the club members know already, right? It's not like Gillette canceled all their memberships and is using this ad to get them to sign back up. Nobody left the club or refused to sign up because they didn't like the old name, so they're not going to flood in to celebrate the new one. Announcements like this are for press releases, not ads.

If the re-branding campaign had been placed in my hands, I would have written something along the lines of "Get The Best Shave A Man Can Get – Delivered To Your Door". Tough, simple and reminiscent of their famous tag line, while conveying all the necessary information. You look at that and you know that the company understands your problem. They've got your solution and they're not going to waste your time. Gillette's weak copy has opened a window of opportunity. If I were to make better ads focused on the same high value keywords, I'd be able to siphon off their PPC search traffic, getting better value for my money.

The low AEI for their ads makes me wonder if Gillette is more focused more on driving traffic organically. Let's check on their SEO to find out. Here's a screen cap from SpyFu.

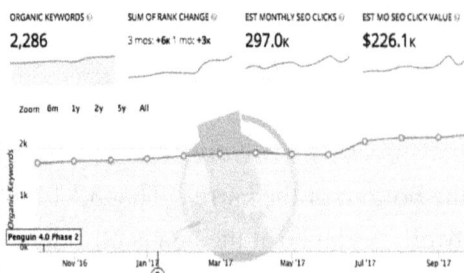

According to this chart, the 2286 organic keywords Gillette On Demand is targeting have a click value of $226,100 per month. In other words, if they had to buy that traffic, that's how much they'd have pay for it. What are these high value, organic keywords?

There they are in blue and white. Gillette is picking up significant traffic from a handful of potent keywords, the majority particular to their brand. They're pushing On Demand as their premiere service, directing searches of the brand name that way. Can you spot the weakness in this approach? Does anything you see in the table above suggest that Gillette is working hard to draw in new customers, those who don't already know and love their brand? With the specific keywords, together with their cost, difficulty and estimated click value, I could chart a course to draw their traffic steadily away.

First I'd structure high quality content around keywords from this list. I'd build landing pages focused on each one and use social media influencers to amplify the noise around my solution. I'd establish a presence on Amazon and move our ranking toward the top. In time, high QS and retention would push me up the Google rankings. For the first few months I'd be chasing Gillette, but unless they raised their game significantly, my growth rate would quickly exceed theirs.

When you examine the competition's data, you're either going to find out that they don't know what they're doing and can safely be ignored, or that they're smart enough that you can learn from what they do well. Either way, knowing how they made their mark will help you make yours faster. I've mentioned disruption several times already. The reality is, most markets you're going to look into are crowded with folks who have a halfway decent idea of how to do their job. To break in, you've got to blow past them, demonstrating a critical difference that will convince customers you know what they love better than anybody else. If you show them that you're prepared to solve their problems, they'll come running, and you'll quickly leave the competition behind.

Case Study: NuPeptin Skin Care

Our case study for this chapter doesn't pit two companies against each other. It's more one vs. the world. The hero is a new skin care line that I recently had the opportunity to launch. It's called NuPeptin. You can read about the Amazon rollout online.[6] What I'm going to talk about here is the process I went through to decide if backing the products under the NuPeptin brand was worth my investment. I'll share the research I did into the market and what looking at the competition showed. To me, the critical factor was whether or not NuPeptin provided a solution in a new and/or different way. I also considered how hard it would be for NuPeptin to break into a crowded market. Keep in mind that at no time in my analysis did I doubt the quality of the brand. The product line is excellent. What I wanted to know was, "Is there room enough in skin care for a high-quality, low-cost brand?"

NuPeptin shares some features with a product called StriVectin, another peptide-based anti-aging skin care brand. Because of differences in formulation and the supply chain for the two brands, NuPeptin products sell for about half

[6]http://www.practicaleCommerce.com/columns/the-eCommerce-corner-office/133204-Using-Amazon-to-launch-NuPeptin-my-new-brand.

the price of a comparable product under StriVectin. This isn't due to a pricing choice I made, it's down to superior logistics. NuPeptin's creams and serums are as effective as the competition's, and they cost the customer much less. Unlike the grocery store brands that cater to a low price point because it's all they know how to do, NuPeptin fills a space that a lot of customers can't afford to reach beyond. Consumers can get by without peptide skin care, it'd just be a shame if they had to.

The first question in front of me when I looked at NuPeptin was, "How big is this market?" To find out, I looked at StriVectin's sales using an Amazon plug-in called Scope. I'm not going to go deep with this plug-in, but a picture's worth a thousand words, right?

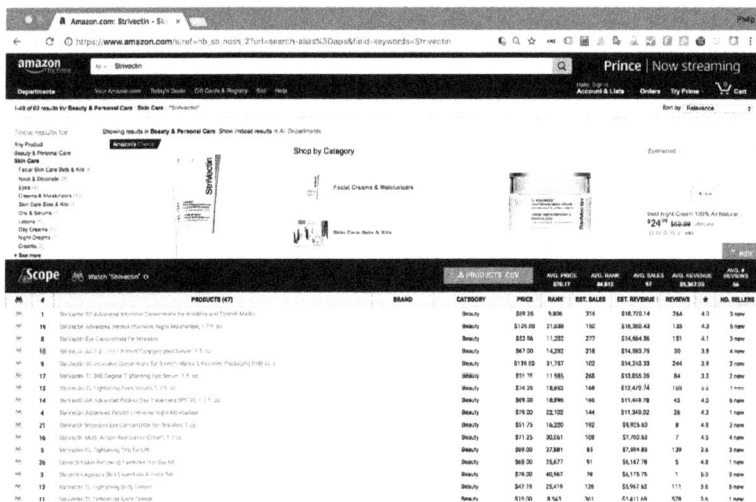

Amazon is a great place to start because it gets a spillover of people who shop mostly online and others who go there just for gifts or products that are harder to find. It's a microcosm that's barely micro these days. As you can see, as of this screenshot, StriVectin was moving close to $200,000 in product per month on Amazon. Among eCommerce sellers who sell on multiple platforms in addition to their own branded sites, like StriVectin does, Amazon represents about 20% of sales at the time of writing. So, figure StriVectin sales at about $1 million per month online. That number doesn't include TV or retail sales. Since I'm looking to sell online, I'm restricting my analysis to the online market. Looking at these numbers, does NuPeptin seem like it'd be a good investment for me? I figure I can capture 10% of that million-dollar market in the short term, so in my analysis, I say it is. Still, there are costs to consider.

What's it going to cost me to put NuPeptin on customers' radars? Thinking about the parameters of the skin care business, who our customers are likely to be and what I already know they respond to, let's see what we can learn from Google AdWords. It's easy. Just type in the key-phrase "Anti Aging Skin Care" and select "Anti-Aging" as a category. This will give us a thumbnail sketch of the field NuPeptin will be playing in. The graph below shows the result of our search.

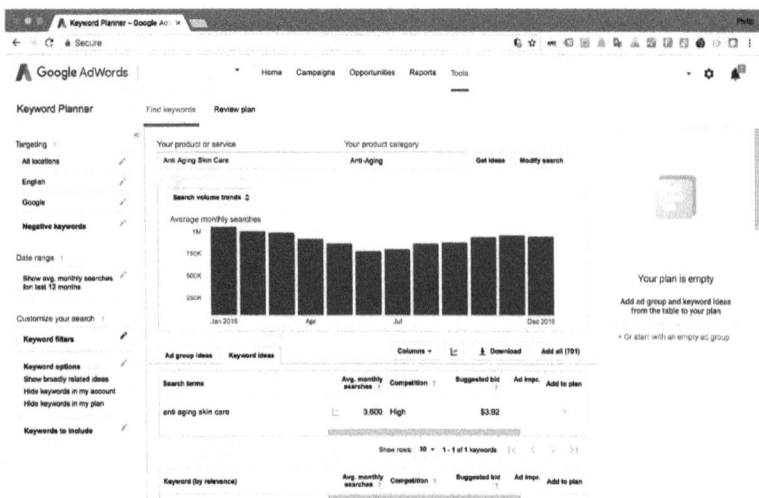

As you can see, search activity is lively around "Anti Aging Skin Care". On Google, it gets between 750,000 and one million searches per month. Looking at the monthly breakdowns, I see that a lot of customers make New Year's Resolutions to protect their skin. I'll file away that observation for future promotions.

Let's branch out. "Anti Aging Skin Care" isn't the only phrase customers search when they're Googling for products like NuPeptin's. What are some others? AdWords is a huge help here, digging deep into Google's algorithms to identify key-phrases that were searched for comparable results. Check out the following suggestions from Keyword Planner.

Pretty nice, right? Google remembers what its millions of users searched for that brought them around to the results page I want to be on, as well as the key-phrases the competition tied together in their metadata. If you showed this kind of data to a marketer from the pre-Internet days, he'd keel over from an aneurysm. And Google gives it away for free!

Looking at the monthly searches of these phrases gives me unbeatable insight into customer behavior. Knowing what people are searching keys us into the problems customers want somebody to solve. Focus groups can't compete with Google's scope, and unlike focus groups, the purchasing data doesn't lie. Google stores so much information on searches, it can tell you more about customer habits than the customers themselves.

My decision to invest in NuPeptin is looking pretty good at this point, but there's one more angle I still want to examine. What is the competition doing to ENGAGE their customers? If there's something they do well, can I do it even better? No market is impossible to crack, but if customer needs are being met to the point that perception of that need is low, changing minds may take more effort than I'm willing to put in. If the competition looks weak, you better believe I'm going to swoop in like a hawk.

For analysis of StriVectin.com, I'm going to turn to SimilarWeb, a paid service that does a good job organizing their data. The next two graphs are from their free section, so you can search StriVectin.com on the site yourself to see how the stats have changed since these screenshots were taken.

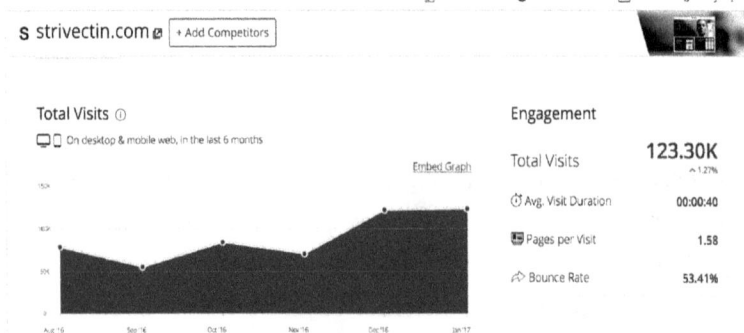

s strivectin.com ☒ + Add Competitors	

Total Visits ⓘ
On desktop & mobile web, in the last 6 months

Embed Graph

Engagement	
Total Visits	**123.30K** ∧ 1.27%
⏱ Avg. Visit Duration	00:00:40
🗐 Pages per Visit	1.58
⌁ Bounce Rate	53.41%

Per this first graph, site traffic at StriVectin.com was holding at about 123,000 site visits per month coming into 2017. On average, an eCommerce site will convert 3.5% of its visits to sales, which gives us a total of 4,305 orders per month. Using the prices of StriVectin's top sellers on Amazon, we can assume an average sale around $70/product, just over $301,350 per month. These are estimates, of course, but what I'm trying to figure out here is where the sales are coming from. Comparing Amazon and site sales to the total market will give me an idea of how much money gets left on the table. Short answer? Plenty.

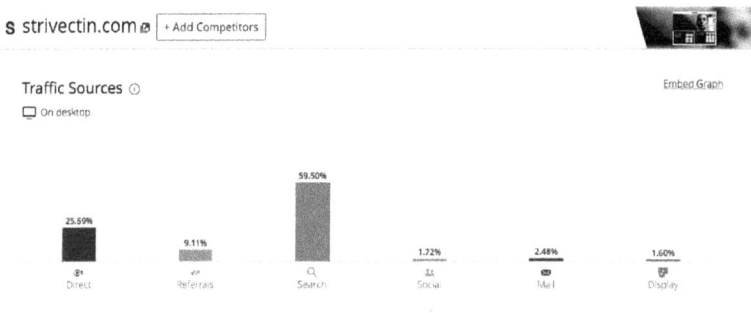

The bar graph above tells me that StriVectin is mostly engaging with customers through search engines and direct hits on their URL. Their content referral is anemic and they're barely a blip on the social media radar. I don't see them using email effectively to retain their customers. This is all great news for me. It means that there's a serious opportunity to engage customers on Instagram, Facebook, Pinterest, etc. I'm confident that by addressing these deficiencies, I can easily steal 10% of StriVectin's sales. NuPeptin has the credentials to deliver as good if not better solutions for the customers we take away. Combine that fact with NuPeptin's price advantage, and I'm confident we can retain those customers.

It's interesting to reflect here on the common sense notion that people have about competition. Most assume that since I'm trying to to launch a new brand, I'm going to view the market leader as my enemy. In reality, I'm happy StriVectin is out there. I'm glad they've done the legwork for me, and I hope they continue to blaze the trail, engaging customers with problems we're both equipped to solve. Every customer who looks at one of their products and says, "If only it were cheaper, I'd buy," is going to love NuPeptin. I've got no problem giving up the fraction of the market that sticks with them out of brand loyalty, so long as my bottom line is going up, up, up.

Take another look at our second SimilarWeb graph. Visits from Direct, Referrals, and Search traffic sources could all have been driven by ads to some extent, so to get a fuller picture of StriVectin's engagement, we need to know if their online ads have been effective in customers' eyes. To get raw data on this, I'll leave SimilarWeb and bring up Follow.net. As a subscriber, I have access to their enhanced offerings, but you can get the updated version of what I'm about to show for free.

The columns we're interested in here are the two dates, which are labeled just above the fold as "First Seen" and "Last Seen". For example, the ad being tracked on line 1 was first seen by a customer on "05-31-2015". It was last seen by a customer on "02-06-2017", very near the date of this screenshot. What does this tell us about the effectiveness of StriVectin's ads?

If an ad runs for a few weeks and is quickly replaced, you know that a savvy marketer was carefully monitoring its performance. The marketer saw that the ad wasn't drawing enough traffic, so they swapped it for something they hoped would be more effective. Ads that run for six months, a year, or more are not so straight forward. It may be that the ad worked great and the marketers decided to leave it out there, doing its work. Or it may be the ad sucks and whatever slacker was supposed to be watching it fell asleep at the wheel. How can you tell a successful long-term campaign from a flop whose marketers have a set-it-and-forget-it mentality?

This is where judgment comes into play. Years of training have taught me how to spot good and bad ads. Even without my experience, the knowledge you get from data mining tools, coupled with common sense, goes a long way. Read through the ads in the screenshot above and ask yourself these questions:

"Is StriVectin using every means available to engage their customers?"

"Are they standing out as better than the competition?"

Something I see right away that StriVectin is missing out on a bit of functionality that Google allows with text ads. The main goal when you're building a text ad is to point out a product's features and benefits. StriVectin's ads do that to some extent, but they also waste a lot of space. Look at ads 1–6 and ad 9. Why does the company bother calling out StriVectin. com on their first line if they're going to give the URL at the bottom? A better use of their character allowance would have been to use up real estate on the page. Remember, customers are going to see this ad in a list of search results, hopefully near the top. A well-built ad will push the competition as far down the page as possible.

Here's an example of what I'm talking about. This is not even one of my own text ads, but I love it all the same. The guys at GhostBed know what they're doing. They call out benefits and clue the customer in to who they are and why they're a great source of solutions. No space is wasted, yet the ad's billboard format leaves an unmissable impression, shoving competing ads south of a typical screen's midline.

GhostBed™ Tax Day Deals - Save On Mattresses & Pillows
[Ad] www.ghostbed.com/Tax-Day/Sales ▾   (866) 343-3354
Over 10,000 reviews & counting. 15 Years in the industry. 101 Night free trial.
Only Natural Latex · Free Shipping & Return · 24 Hour Shipping · Pay Monthly No Credit
Deal: $170 off 2 Free Pillows · Code TAX2

Get 2 Free GhostPillows   **GhostBed™ Reviews**
Tax Day Promo. Save $175   See why our customers trust us with
2 Free Pillows with King & Queen.   their comfort.

See how the structure of this ad helps it stand out? Some people mix up flashy and effective. GhostBed isn't going for fireworks here. Fireworks aren't what their customers are after. Rather, GhostBed is using their text allowance to maximize their messaging and minimize opportunities for their competition. If StriVectin isn't familiar with this basic technique, I'm confident I can get NuPeptin's text ads to come out on top.

What about banner ads? Am I going to have trouble catching up to the lead StriVectin has on eye-catching visuals? Follow.net gives us a look at what they've been doing.

I'm not seeing anything to worry me here. StriVectin's ads are info dumps without a lot of verve. That's not to say they aren't decent informational ads, it's just clear that StriVectin isn't in the middle of some high-concept campaign that I'm going to have a hard time countering. The fact that these ads don't have more going on despite their longevity suggests that StriVectin isn't making a push to engage new customers, at least not online. Digital marketing isn't their top priority, which means it's a good time to enter the field.

By the time this book lands, I'm sure there'll be new wrinkles to the NuPeptin saga. Google "Anti Aging Skin Care" to see how we're doing. Check us out on Amazon, SimilarWeb, and Follow.net. I wouldn't be surprised if you saw a dip in StriVectin's market share, but my main goal at this point is to carve out a tenth of the existing pie, then grow the pie. I don't think that's going to be a problem. NuPeptin is a great solution to an enduring beauty need and I'm just the guy to get the word out. Those are two good reasons to feel confident about my investment.

5 – Adjust Your Pitch

The biggest determiner of whether your business succeeds or fails is always going to be knowing your customer. You have to know who they are and what they love. Then and only then can you sell to them effectively. When I say that all you need to know about marketing is THINK ENGAGE THRIVE, that's what I'm talking about. Anybody can look at demographics. A car manufacturer can look at who's buying cars and say, "My ideal customer is between the ages of twenty-nine and forty-five. They're married with a combined income between sixty and eighty thousand dollars. They've got 1.5 kids, two goldfish, and a dog." But that doesn't help sell cars. In fact, it's totally meaningless, because even if it accurately describes the statistics, it says nothing about how to connect with customers on an emotional level. Without that connection, you can't drive sales and build retention.

Data and the modern tools that help you comb through data give more and better insight into customer behavior than all the demographics, focus groups, outdated model analysis, and academic definitions in history. As I've emphasized in our Useful Tools sections, looking at data from a few different angles is critical to understanding how to ENGAGE. If you THINK and ENGAGE, your business will THRIVE, achieving new levels of success that will allow you to reinvest in the continuing cycle.

Tightrope walkers fifty feet off the ground look straight ahead, not down. Their training tells them that the body follows the head, so they learn to adjust their balance constantly by the feel of the cable. As strong and rigid as it may appear, no cable is perfectly still. The movements of the walker send ripples up and down its length. Winds buffet it. Subtle motions of its anchors make it sway. Markets are like that cable. Even the most outwardly stable move with the flow of customer opinion, competitive pressure, and social fluctuations. Who would have predicted that a generation raised on Harry Potter would carry enough nostalgia for printed books to keep publishing viable in the era of tablets and smartphones? The point is, markets change. Like a walker on a tightrope, you have to keep looking ahead, shifting at the speed of thought. The alternative is a swift fall.

I've already mentioned the need for constant attention to your web presence. Look at the data. Be responsive. Sometimes you're going to be surprised by the trends. Sometimes a stunt or a gimmick you were sure was going to take off will sink like a lead balloon. At times like this you have to take a step back. You're not married to your ideas. If you're willing to change, you'll often find that your marketing isn't broken, just malfunctioning. Small adjustments may be all that's needed to lift an idea out of the dust and send it flying.

Success comes back to the central question, "What do my customers love?" Everything you do should be guided by your answer to that question. When you've taken a customer-focused approach and something still goes wrong, it's time to look deeper. Ask, "Why do my customers love what they love?" Unlike our central question, this one has a definite answer. Customers are aspirational. Their nature – human nature – is to want to go someplace else, do something else, be somebody else. We all want to be special, to feel important. And why not? Every public defender is the star of her own courtroom drama, every dad pushing a stroller around the mall is his kid's Superman. Great companies solve customer problems. If people are defined by the ambitions they pursue, the greatest good a company can do is to help customers reach for their goals.

How to Sell a Size Fourteen

One facet of my past marketing was selling products on the Home Shopping Network. I had worked on several clothing lines targeted at different lifestyles. One line designed for women of a certain age who reflect the reality of the American body type. The designer had developed the line to cover up a woman's "icky bits." Everybody has icky bits, even people who get paid to look good on TV, so we were confident the line would be popular.

The average dress size of a woman in this country is between twelve and fourteen. Compare this to a box-office bombshell or supermodel at size six or below. If you were a traditional marketer putting together a 4P plan, you might think, "Our customer is a woman over fifty. She's size fourteen, with a household income of $75,000. So we need to show our clothes on size-fourteen models. Each piece should cost no more than $50, since that's what our customer can afford. We'll sell our product to discount retailers." That plan would be an epic failure. Customers would flip channels on impulse, shaking their heads that we could be so out of touch. Average-sized clothes on average-sized models are not what people want to see, and they certainly won't vote with their dollars to have them stick around.

Nobody aspires to be average. Fashion customers at HSN, like fashion customers everywhere, want to look slim and feel beautiful. To sell them clothes you don't give them a visual that matches who they are. You show them who they aspire to be. That's why we chose to show our icky-bit camouflaging line on size-six models. Age was a factor, too. It would have made no sense to show the line on models who looked fifty. I didn't mind if fifty was their actual age, but I needed them to look thirty-five. Thirty-five fits the aspiration of a fifty-year-old woman. She doesn't want to look like a teenager. But an attractive, sophisticated woman who carries herself with confidence and knows how to dress? That's who these ladies want smiling back at them from mirror.

If you want to sell size-fourteen clothes to a fifty-year-old woman, you show those clothes on a size-six, thirty-five-year-old model. If you were to ask the customer what kind of ad she'd respond to in a focus group, she'd lie to your face. "I want to see real clothes on real women," she'd say. Sure. Try it sometime. See how many pant suits and weekend jeans you sell parading pear-shaped grandmas in a slow circle. It's a harsh reality, but it's true. Average doesn't sell. Forget the focus groups. At HSN, we showed clothes designed for women with average American bodies on models half their size. The line sold out.

It's not just clothes that work this way. Listings for skin care products will tell you that they remove fine lines and wrinkles, scrub away dead skin, cover blemishes. But those aren't the features I'd call out in ads. Customers don't ENGAGE with removing and covering. They ENGAGE with looking good, feeling good. So sell youth. Sell them rejuvenation. That's what gets them excited, that gets them to buy. Successful skin care lines sell products that make customers look good.

There's Such a Thing as Too Beautiful

RAW Essentials started as an online and shopping channel brand, exclusively marketed on HSN in 2008. My partner in the business was Carol Alt. As a supermodel, one look told you she knew something about the beauty business. After I read up on her lifestyle, I started getting excited about her expertise. Carol is a raw food enthusiast who has written books on the subject. She believes wholeheartedly that 100% natural is the way to go in diet and skin care, so she was the perfect person to advise and promote our brand. Talk about congruity!

Similar to the deal I'd later work out with Michael Phelps in my 800Razors.com days, Carol was not just an endorser of the product, but a part owner. Her good name was tied into the reception the brand was going to get as a product line. Nothing motivates like having skin in the game. So when we launched RAW Essentials, I was confident we were about to have a hit on our hands. But nothing's ever easy. Celebrity endorsements are tricky, as I've already illustrated.

Our first shows on HSN went okay. We didn't knock it out of the park, but did enough business to continue. One advantage of Direct To Consumer advertising, the method practiced by HSN, is that it puts you in contact with the customer at the point of sale. Even before we went off the air, we started to get feedback on what we were doing. It turned out people didn't love it. Complaints came in that Carol seemed unapproachable. Her supermodel looks came across as over-the-top, a little intimidating. This wasn't a complete shock to me, as I'd observed other models on the shopping channels deliberately dressing down. I talked to Carol about this, and after sharing the customer comments, she agreed to tone down her look.

Our customers wanted to believe that the beauty products we were selling would make them look younger, eliminate fine lines and wrinkles. They saw Carol and said to themselves, "I could never look like that." It hurt their aspirational self-image to have the bar set so high. Plus, they heard Carol advocating her healthy, raw lifestyle and thought, "Am I going to have to change my whole life to get the benefit?" We put Carol in basic hair and makeup, changed her wardrobe to a polo shirt and khakis, and modified her message. Instead of talking about her lifestyle, she focused on the solution we were selling. Retinol is a familiar brand of acid that burns away four levels of skin, temporarily eliminating the appearance of wrinkles. Our key product was a healthy alternative that used vitamin A from carrots to nourish the skin instead of stripping it away. We had to sell it hard because it took longer to show results than Retinol, but by presenting our customers with the real Carol that was usually hidden under glitz and glam, we broke through. Customers saw that they could aspire to be like our lovely spokesperson. We engaged, so they bought.

On the website, we took the same approach, talking less about lifestyle, more about skin cream. We told customers what the product did, how it differed from the harmful chemicals that gave inferior results. We explained that because our creams and serums were raw, we didn't cook away the vitamins and antioxidants. There were no preservatives and no toxins. You could have spread any of our products on a cracker or sprayed them on a salad, though I can't vouch for the taste. Online success was important for us. It was difficult to get traction against Oil of Olay and L'Oreal. Their deep pockets and aggressive marketing made it very difficult for us to rank on the first page of a Google search. The fact that we were on

HSN was great because it got our name out there. These days, when customers hear something new, their first impulse is to Google it. So HSN sales were only part of our total package. Once they knew our name, they checked the website. Those customers who hadn't quite been convinced by Carol saw a product the competition couldn't match. We won them over with solutions. When you're launching a new brand, half the battle is getting your product seen by customers. Every time RAW Essentials appeared on HSN, we'd see a surge of customers researching us online. We built up quickly thanks to this exposure.

How can you achieve similar results if you don't have access to a shopertainment channel like HSN? The simple answer, and the one that always makes financial sense, is to launch on Amazon. Customers are nervous about giving an unknown company their credit card number. They shop at Amazon because they know Amazon. They know that if something goes wrong with their transaction, Amazon will back them up.

Spot Cost versus Product Cost

A more expensive but still highly effective way to get people familiar with your brand is through TV commercials. Online is the future, but low cost of entry makes for a lot of crowding on the edge of AdSense-enabled pages. Broadcast and cable TV ads can catch and keep customers' attention. Common knowledge would say that TV ads are too expensive for a company just starting out, but that's an oversimplification.

While operating 800Razors.com, I learned a lot about TV commercials. Salesmen in that industry talk a lot about CPM, or "Cost Per Mile", where a mile represents one thousand viewers. They try to sell you high dollar spots by telling you the CPM is worth it. Don't listen. The smart buy in TV time is remnant television, the industry's equivalent of on-call air travel. Remnant doesn't hold out the promise of high viewership, but when you compare spot cost to product cost, it's much easier to make the numbers work out.

Consider the alternative. You could buy time on Fox Business or NFL Today, spending $5000 for a 30-second commercial. I guarantee that unless you're already a major brand, you'll never make that money back. I don't think even the top brands are profiting off those spots. Nobody's going to sell $10,000 worth of product off a single $5000 ad. Contrast that with buying a remnant ad on one of the lesser-known channels, places like Fox Sports 2. That high up the dial, a thirty second spot might cost you as little as $10. If you were selling a $20 product at a 50% margin, all you'd have to do to cover costs is make one sale. When I was buying ads for 800Razors.com, our average sale was $27, so a single sale on a $10 ad was enough to turn a profit. I didn't care when the ad aired. A two-in-the-morning spot was still going to make me one sale.

During this period, I bought time on Fox Business during the wee hours. Thirty seconds alongside Maria Bartiromo would have cost me $5000, but in the dead of night, $250 was enough for a remnant slot. To justify that expense, we had to make 25 sales. Thanks to FBN's bigger audience share, we did. After that, we bounced around to different networks and different times, but success always came down to slot cost relative to product cost.

That's the key to television. Forget about CPMs. Ignore the guys who say, "Don't think about day one sales. Wait ten weeks for the turn around." Get a cheap spot wherever you can. If it costs you $50 and you do $50 in sales, decide if the hassle was worth it. If one spot makes money, try more. If not, back off. It took me two years and millions of advertising dollars to learn that lesson. Anybody in direct response television will tell you the same thing. Spot cost versus product cost is all you need to know.

Don't Stop at Thrive

Whatever method or medium you chose to get the word out on your brand, the steps you take to liftoff are the same. You have to identify your customers, find out what they love, sell them solutions, run the numbers, adjust your pitch...and repeat. THINK ENGAGE THRIVE is a cycle. I can't emphasize that enough. If marketing is everything you do to get customers to buy your product, then a marketer is a person whose job it is to connect with customers in order to get them to buy. That connection, that engagement, is the beating heart of the consumer economy. It's the driving principle every business needs to understand.

You can't sell without engaging, so every sale is proof that you're doing a good job. However, it's when fledgling companies start to THRIVE that many take their first steps toward eating dirt. High on their own early success, they stop disrupting, stop innovating. Instead of thinking about customers, they start to follow the competition. Like the supermarkets discussed in Chapter 1, or Blackberry from Chapter 2, they lose focus. They try to do what the other guy does. Maybe they do it cheaper. That gives them a little traction. Then the market corrects as customers see they're not offering anything new. Suddenly the only way to go is down. How can you avoid this trap? By being flexible, always ready to move with the tide.

My discovery of the shave brush guy using one of my razors, mentioned in Chapter 3, confirmed a suspicion I'd had for awhile, that subscriptions like the one sold at 800Razors. com were in for a rocky road ahead. In our case, the problem was that one person might use two razors a month, while somebody else may burn through six. This averages out to the four razors our subscription service was targeting, but it doesn't perfectly solve the problem of either customer. The guy whose blade doesn't dull so fast is going to start questioning why he's paying to get twice as many replacements as he needs delivered. The lady who insists on a fresh, keen edge every time she shaves will get annoyed at us when she has to pick up extra blades at retail prices. Neither is going to be satisfied because both are getting less value for their money.

A similar dilemma forced Birchbox to make dramatic changes to their subscriptions. Early on, people loved getting new boxes every month. They felt like they were getting a gift. Birchbox's original model was based on the idea that subscribers would enjoy their four or five samples from the box, then go to the company website and buy the full sizes of their favorites. That was never going to work. After a few months, many customers had collected enough samples that a full size of anything would have just been taking up space in their medicine cabinets. They got sick of unneeded gifts and canceled in droves. Birchbox saw the writing on the wall and announced plans to open brick-and-mortar stores. That deal fell through and the company went through successive rounds of layoffs. Time will tell if they're able to adjust fast enough to save their brand.

Blue Apron is another company that is attempting to disrupt by means of online ordering, this time in the food industry. The trouble I see with their model is that food is time-sensitive. Sure, a customer might be willing to go for a Blue Apron meal a few nights a week, but the concept is built around planning ahead, deciding exactly what you want to cook well in advance. It's a time-saver for well-ordered minds. For the rest of us, it won't be long before we start complaining there's nothing in the fridge we want. Blue Apron is going up against our God-given right to microwave a pizza on a night we're supposed to be sautéing sugar peas. They've tackled the meal problem without dealing with impulse buys. I know from experience that's not going to work. My wife likes the flavor of muscadines, but she hates spitting out seeds. Every so often she'll get a craving and make a purchase. A week later, half a container of fat, purple grapes will go out with the trash.

Multiply the Muscadine Effect by the size of your typical grocery order and you'll see what I mean. Not only is Blue Apron asking customers to plan out a week's worth of meals, they're expecting people to suppress their cravings for comfort dishes. If you don't resist the urge to run our to a restaurant or the store, ingredients are going to mount up. Blue Apron's prices are too high for the majority of shoppers, anyway. They're targeting the 10% of shoppers who happen to be both health-conscious and well-to-do. It's hard to make money when you're selling to a subset.

If the supermarkets knew anything about marketing, they'd jump in the food box business and drive everybody out. With their supply chains, they could keep prices low. The convenience of their locations makes home delivery such a luxury that most folks wouldn't miss it. Stores could pack up ingredient boxes for different days of the week and people would stop in on their way home from work to pick them up. Does all of the above mean Blue Apron is doomed? Not necessarily. They're a young company who managed to make a lot of noise before the flaws in their plan became obvious. With enough investment, maybe they can address their weaknesses. I am skeptical, though. Food doesn't seem a good fit for an online subscription service. In America, you can always count on finding cheap food and cheap gas. Any company trying to shake things up while raising prices is going to run into a perception problem.

Here's the point. Businesses that THRIVE don't follow the competition. They read data, using what they find out to get closer to the customer. Their products solve customer problems and their service makes buying that solution a positive experience. THINK ENGAGE THRIVE is all you need to know about marketing because engagement equals sales. When you offer a solution nobody can match, price doesn't matter. Competition doesn't matter. A fully engaged company is bulletproof. I've mentioned several companies that fit that description, including Apple, Amazon, and Dunkin' Donuts.

The Road Ahead

My own latest endeavor, Hound Dog Digital, got off the ground after I sold 800Razors.com. There were plenty of avenues I could have gone down, so the decision to concentrate on digital marketing came about because of demand. People were coming up to me, saying, "While you're figuring out your next move, feel free to help me with my eCommerce." It was a joke based on truth. I knew eCommerce inside and out. Finding clients who knew enough about my history to trust me with their businesses was no problem. Since opening our virtual doors, we've been able to expand in a big way, picking up new clients every month. Our specialty is the Amazon marketplace. There's a huge demand and we're very good at what we do. Customers come to us wanting help to launch their brand. We tell them how to optimize their product pages, how to list, how to market and get sales.

Amazon is its own little world. They have their own SEO, which a lot of people don't understand. There are many companies serving "Amazon services", but they aren't really our competitors. What they're selling is logistics. We're selling expertise. Get your product in Amazon's warehouse is the easy part. It's not what most businesses are looking to buy. What matters to them is, "How can I sell?" At Hound Dog Digital, we sell solutions to the selling problem. That's why we're able to attract Fortune 100 companies to our client list. Not all our clients are millionaires, of course. They don't all have a venture capitalist's phone number in their back pockets. Making noise on social media is one way we draw attention to what they're doing and doing well. We get the attention of customers, and in some cases, like that of my guitar string innovating friend, we get the competition to stand up and take notice, too. Our PPC, SEO, and marketing strategy is second to none. As of October 2017 we're on track to close out our first full calendar year with $1 million in revenue, and we're just getting started.

If I can make successes of business after business, what's stopping you? Decades of experience have prepared me to be flexible, able to jump from one challenge to the next, but no matter how many times my companies have faced an uncertain future, the key to pushing through has always been THINK ENGAGE THRIVE. You know your business better than anybody else. You know your strengths and you know how to avoid your weaknesses. You know that your solution is the best. Now that your focus is firmly on customers and you understand the value of data, you're ready to sell your message to the masses. Nothing's stopping you. Nothing can. Identify your customers, find out what they love, sell them solutions, run the numbers, and adjust your pitch. The road ahead is hazy, but it's as long as you want to make it. Now is the time to put organic marketing to work for you.

9 Steps to Think- Engage -Thrive Marketing Success

THINK

Step 1 – Everything Begins With The Customer

Customers are the foundation of any business. Without them, you have no business.

To connect with yours, make sure you know them intimately so you can build your marketing programs around their needs, wants, and loves.

You have been provided with many tools to learn about what cus- tomers are doing and what they are looking for. Keyword Planners, Google Trends, Social Media all provide tangible insight into the customer. Think about what you see in this data and build a customer personality framework for your business.

Here are some fundamental questions you need to be able to answer about your business.

Who is your customer?

Why do they need your product?

What is the key benefit the customer gets from using your product? What can you say about your business that the competition cannot? What inspires the customer?

What will bring them to your brand?

Your business is ultimately about them, so start off on the right foot and get to know them before they even walk in the door, so to speak.

Step 2 – Develop Your Strategic Marketing Framework

Think about this for a minute.

Average marketers think in terms of weekly campaigns.
Great marketers think in terms of an overall strategy.

Your strategy guides your marketing campaigns. Each campaign should be focused on the following goals:

- Awareness
- Engagement
- Retention

When developing your marketing strategy, focus your campaigns and budget to address these three goals. Keep in mind that awareness and engagement mean little if you can't keep your customers around after their first purchase.

How much of your budget will you allocate to awareness campaigns? How much to engagement?

How much to retention?

For consumer product companies we recommend an allocation of 25% Awareness

50% Engagement

25% Retention

For B2B companies we recommend 40% Awareness

40% Engagement

20% Retention

Step 3 – Develop Your Brand Story

What is your Brand Story?

Brand storytelling is the WHY of your company.

Why do the customers need you and what value do they get from your brand?

Why does your company exist?

Don't confuse your brand story with your company summary. Your brand story is about your customers. It is an important step in mar- keting because it will determine your brand voice and how you will speak to your customers.

Your story will guide your brand's website, social, and content strat- egy as well as your overall marketing messaging.

If your customers see you as a young hip brand, your content will be written in that voice. If you are a serious brand, then you will want to communicate in a serious voice. The best marketers figure out ways to get the customers to tell their brand story.

Two great examples of using customers for your brand storytelling are Weightwatchers and Proactive. When you review their website, content, video and social strategies, you can see a cohesive storytell- ing strategy from a customers perspective.

Develop your story, and let your customers own it.

Step 4 – Build Your Presence

You have defined your customer and you know them intimately. You have your marketing strategy planned and you have built your brand story. It is now time to use this information to build your website, social media pages, and advertising.

You want all of these customer touch points to have a coordinated look, feel, and messaging to your customers. Even your 404 Error pages can be put to use to show off your attention to detail.

Whether you are consumer focused or business-to-business, hire a user experience designer. They will take your customer profile, your marketing goals and your brand story to create a design and flow that helps convert visits to buyers.

Begin with the mobile experience first. How will you be able to express your brand on a mobile phone or tablet. It is always easier to expand content and add features for a desktop experience than it is to take away unnecessary elements for mobile. When you think about the customer today, mobile it becoming the first screen.

ENGAGE

Step 5 – Get Traffic To Your Site

Once you understand your brand's reason for being and have built your site, it's time to engage. Here are a few basic ways to get traffic and customers to your site.

Paid Advertising – There are plenty of paid advertising opportunities online and offline. The most common online are Google AdWords, Bing and Yahoo, which are keyword driven text ads. There are also keyword driven display ads, content driven native ads, retargeting ads and direct buy ads to name a few.

This can be a very effective awareness building and engagement channel. Paid advertising is also highly measurable so carefully track your spend and Return on Ad Spend (ROAS) in each campaign.

Search Engine Optimization – SEO is a highly effective engage- ment method using online search traffic. Your objective is to be the first response when customers are asking questions online related to what you sell. This is one of the best engagement channels as customers are searching for the solution that you provide. This is a lot of work, requires SEO expertise and is an ongoing effort. But when done correctly, it is the most profitable method.

Social Media – Social Media is not about directly selling. This is the biggest mistake brands make. Remember your brand story? This is where you want to use that story to start conversations with customers. Engage with your customers in a way that reinforces why they should buy from you.

Here is a way that I like to explain social strategy to my clients. Think about social media as a party that you have been invited to with thousands of guests whom you don't know. Would you begin a conversation with someone by handing out coupons for $5 off or are you going to strike up conversations and get to know the others at the party?

Social media gives you the chance to really connect and engage with your customers. Reinforce why you are the brand that they should love. When executed correctly, this is a very effective awareness and retention channel.

Email - Build your email list through purchases and visitors to your website. Getting a customer to purchase is the best way. But not all visitors to your site will purchase. Be creative to get your visitors to provide an email. Give something away to get an email from a visitor. These are people who have shown interest in your product.

Buying a list is ineffective and costly. We never recommend this method. These are lists of people who have shown no interest in your brand, and conversions will be very low. Your own hard-won email list is the most effective retention and engagement channel.

Display – Display ads are most suitable for awareness building. When you know your customer very well, you will know the types of sites they will visit. You can use display ads on those sites to remain in their purchase consideration set. However, don't expect a lot of engagement from these ads. They won't generate orders but they will get your brand message out and increase awareness.

These are the basic traffic generating methods. Once you have mastered these, there are many more. We have a list of 110 Traffic

Building Methods for your Website on www.hounddogdigital. com that will give you other ideas for building your site traffic.

Step 6 – Conversion Optimization

Getting traffic to your site is costly and hard work. You want to make the most of it.

In this book, we have provided 110 Great Digital Marketing Tools. Several of those tools are focused on conversion optimization for your website and your advertising campaigns. You should continually measure and optimize all of your traffic generating sources.

Many first time e-commerce entrepreneurs are surprised at the conversion rates they can expect on their website. When we explain that for every one hundred website visitors you can expect 3 orders, they are shocked. Certainly, there are sites getting conversions in the double digits, but they have been in business for a long time, have a specialized product and have defined their customer with a bull's-eye.

This is the reason we spend so much time working on site optimiza- tion methods. As an online brand you want to make the best return on your traffic driving spend. This takes time, effort and skill.

Here is a list of the most recent average conversion rates by industry.

Auto Products	2.27%
B2B	2.58%
Consumer Services	5.00%

Dating & Personals	2.75%
E-commerce	2.91%
Education	4.13%
Employment Services	3.97%
Finance & Insurance	7.19%
Health & Medical	2.51%
Home Goods	3.68%
Industrial Services	2.58%
Legal	4.35%
Real Estate	4.40%
Technology	2.55%
Travel & Hospitality	2.57%

When you consistently test, measure, and tweak, your conversion rates can be optimized to a much higher percentage than these aver- ages. Also, knowing exactly who your customer is and how best to engage with them, will increase your site above the average.

Step 7 – Affiliate Marketing

Affiliate marketing is an often-overlooked segment of digital mar- keting and it can be highly effective for any kind of brand. It is a performance-based process, which rewards the affiliates for each visit, customer, or order brought to the brand by the affiliate's mar- keting efforts.

Affiliates are simply other websites that advertise your product and are paid a bounty based on the agreed conversion. Affiliate ads can be anything from text links to extravagant skyscraper banners provided by you.

There are four parts to affiliate marketing. It begins with the brand or retailer; the network that manages the affiliates and the payments; the affiliate or publisher who lists your deal on their site; lastly is the consumer who takes advantage of the deal.

Affiliate marketing should average about 15% of your total web sales. This channel will grow as your brand grows and it can be a profitable channel when managed correctly.

THRIVE

Step 8 – Retention Marketing

Now that you have created a marketing system to continually deliver site visits and customers, you need to protect what you have built. Don't make the mistake of taking customers for granted and believing they will always return.

Retention marketing is a discipline founded in continual communi- cation with your customers. The two best methods to employ in this channel are email and social media. These are your retention touch points and also enable you to advertise new offers to well-qualified leads.

There are auto responder emails systems that will automate this process and provide measurable and actionable retention statistics. Our favorite product is by Windsor Circle, which has quickly become a standard in the e-commerce industry.

Step 9 - Reviews

Reviews are essential to your success online. This cannot be understated.

Consider that 90% of consumers read reviews BEFORE visiting a site. So having your reviews on unbiased third party sites like Google, Amazon, Yelp, or TrustPilot is essential to thriving.

Here are a few more statistics to reinforce the point.

- 88% of consumers trust reviews as much as personal recommendations.

- 72% of customers will take action after reading positive reviews.

- Customers spend 31% more with companies that have ex- cellent reviews.

- 86% of customers will not visit a site with negative reviews.

These 9 steps, when executed correctly, will set your digital market- ing on a solid foundation and allow your business to Thrive.

For an evaluation of your site and business or to schedule Phil Ma- siello for a speaking engagement visit www.PhilMasiello. com for contact information.

110 Great Digital Marketing Tools

Below is a list of marketing tools that can help e-commerce business owners promote their products or services online. These tools will also help business owners devise strategies in light of the results or analysis derived from some of these tools.

These tools have been derived with the help of using various sources available online.

Customer Engagement Tools

1. **Hub Spot CRM** – A powerful tool to manage your CRM – free - https://www.hubspot.com/

2. **Typeform** – Engage your visitors using popup forms – free - https:// www.typeform.com/

3. **SurveyMonkey** – obtain valuable feedback from customers using surveys – free - https://www.surveymonkey.com/

4. **Inselly** – A solution for selling products on Instagram – free - http:// inselly.com/

5. **Charlie** – Find multiple social profiles of people you meet – free - https://charlieapp.com/

6. **Rebrandly** – Shorten your URL to make it look more credible – free - https://www.rebrandly.com/

7. **Segment** – Collect customer data from multiple sources and manage it using one account – Free - https://segment.com/

8. **Wistia** – Promote and manage business' promotional videos with content control option – free - https://wistia.com/welcomeback

9. **Word Press** – Design free websites or blog pages with easy-to-use designs and themes – free - https://wordpress.com/

10. **Medium** – A platform to share blogs and articles with millions of readers – free - https://medium.com/

11. **Peek** – Get feedback about your website or app from real people through video based interviews – free - http://peek.usertesting.com/

12. **Hub Spot's Blog Topic Generator** – Generate multiple blog topics using your keywords for your businesses' SEO or Content Market- ing – free - https://www.hubspot.com/blog-topic-generator

13. **Content Idea Generator** – Generate creative ideas for your articles and web content – free - http://www.contentideagenerator.com/

14. **Go Squared** – Convert your visitors in real time using Go Squared's Chat software – 14 Day Free Trial - https://www.gosquared.com/

15. **Hello Bar** – Attract your customers by designing messages for them – Free - https://www.hellobar.com/

16. **Blogger** – Publish your blogs which will be accessible to millions of readers – free - https://www.blogger.com/about/

17. **YouTube** - A video sharing website accessible globally – free -https://www.youtube.com/

18. **Vimeo** – Share promotional or informational videos for generating traffic for your website and app – free - https://vimeo.com/

19. **Similar Web** – Identify leading marketing trends - free - https:// www.similarweb.com/

Email Marketing Service

20. **Benchmark Email** – Online email marketing tool used to increase customer engagement – free - https://www. benchmarkemail. com/?p=598262

21. **Mail Chimp** – organize and send bulk emails to facilitate your e-commerce business – free - https://mailchimp. com/

22. **SendinBlue** – Send newsletters, bulk emails and SMS to facilitate your marketing efforts – free for 9000 emails - https://www.send- inblue.com/?AID=12280511&PID=796 7975&SID=/

23. **Mailjet** – All–in-one email marketing tool – free 6000 emails per month - https://www.mailjet.com/

24. **Mailgun** – email management API for sending and receiving emails free - https://www.mailgun.com/

Competitor Research

25. **HeatSync** – attain competitor analysis for better decision making free - http://r.hsync.us/NTY4NDQ1-1933+6.php

26. **KeywordSpy** – Free competitors' PPC & SEO keyword search software – free -http://www.keywordspy.com/

27. **Follow** – Get detailed insights of your competitor's website – free - http://follow.net/

28. **Spyfu-** allows you to spy on keywords competitors are using - Start- ing at $33/month https://www.spyfu.com/

Social Sharing

29. **Flare** – add a widget to your blog or content, enabling visitors to share it on their social profiles – free - https://wordpress.org/plugins/ flare/

30. **AddThis** – make your content shareable by adding widgets – free - http://www.addthis.com/

31. **Social Plugins** – allows your customers to save, like and share your website content on Facebook – free - https://developers.facebook. com/docs/plugins

32. **LinkedIn Plugins** – Add LinkedIn widgets to your website content free - https://developers.facebook.com/docs/plugins

33. **Pinterest Goodies** – helps in pinning and sharing your work – free - https://about.pinterest.com/en/browser-button

Keyword Research

34. **Google Trends** – Research top ranking keywords to enhance your content – free - https://trends.google.com/trends/

35. **Internet Marketing Ninjas** - an on page optimization tool. free - https://www.internetmarketingninjas.com/seo-tools/ free-optimization/

36. **WordStream** – A frequently updated database with millions of keywords and long-tail keywords – free -http://www.wordstream. com/free-keyword-tools

37. **Ubersuggest** – Find the latest keywords not updated in Google keyword planner – free -https://ubersuggest.io/

38. **Keyword Tool** –The best alternative to Google Keyword Planner, receive over 750+ keywords – free -http://keywordtool.io/

39. **Google Keyword Planner** – Research top trending keywords   to optimize your content – free - http://adwords.google.com/ keywordplanner

40. **Alexa** – Receive top keywords and competitor analysis to enhance your content – 7 Day Free Trial - http://www.alexa.com/

41. **SEMrush** – find out the best keywords for your website – 7 Day Free Trialhttps://www.semrush.com/sem/

DIY Graphic Tools

42. **Canva** – Graphic designing and editing tool for your blogs, graphics, presentations, etc – Free -https://www.canva.com/

43. **Pablo** –Design engaging images for your posts – free - https:// pablo.buffer.com/

SEO Tools

44. **SEO Bin** – allows you to optimize your title tags and meta descrip- tion tags – free -http://seobin.org/

45. **Snippet Optimizer** – Preview how your link appears on search engines to make adequate changes – free - http:// snippetoptimizer. net/

46. **Microsoft Free SEO Toolkit** –Review and enhance your SEO content for better search ranking – free - https:// www.microsoft. com/web/seo

47. **SEOBook** – Check your content for SEO and limit excessive keyword density – free - http://tools.seobook.com/general/ keyword-density/

48. **Screaming Frog** – This tool is a website crawler that helps your URLs to crawl better – free - https://www. screamingfrog.co.uk/ seo-spider/

49. **WebCEO** – Get a detailed SEO report of your website to im- prove content quality – 14 Day Free Trial - https:// www.webceo. com/?id=12264

50. **Lipperhey** – It analyzes quality, searchability and popularity of your website – free - https://www.lipperhey. com/en/

51. **GeoRanker** – Get accurate real-time local SERP Rankings Reports free - https://www.georanker.com/

52. **Open Site Explorer** – SEO optimization tool for website back- linking and link building – 30 Day Free Trial - https://moz.com/ researchtools/ose/

53. **SEO PowerSuite** – Easy to use SEO tools to promote your website free -http://www.sps-software.net/

54. **Google Tag Manager** –Optimize and manage website tags for better SEO – free - https://www.google.com/ analytics/tag-manager/

Lead Generation

55. Sumo – A tool that helps increase your website's traffic – free - https://sumo.com/

56. Rapportive - generate LinkedIn leads by receiving relevant profiles in your Gmail - Free - https://rapportive.com/

57. Voila Norbert – Generates 50 corporate leads – free - https://www. voilanorbert.com/

Social Media Management and Analytics

58. Buffer – share the page you are reading easily – Free for 1 user https://buffer.com/

59. Conversion Score – Discover your social media conversion rate free - https://www.socialbakers.com/statistics/facebook/pages/ detail/137157819756765-conversation-score

60. SharedCount – Find out how many followers, shares and likes you have on each social media platform – free - http://www.sharedcount. com/

61. SumAll – Monitor your business and social media metrics – free - https://sumall.com/

62. Hootsuite – manage all your social media accounts from one app free - https://hootsuite.com/

63. Social Analytics – Collect and analyze statistical online data – free - https://getsocialanalytics.com/index.html

64. Socialbakers – the most accurate social media analytics and reporting tool – free -https://www.socialbakers.com/suite/ social-media-analytics-and-reporting

65. **Latergramme** – schedule Instagram posts for better visibility – free - https://later.com/

66. **Quintly** – Optimize your social media performance by tracking and benchmarking – 14 Day Free Trial - https://www.quintly.com/

Content Optimization

67. **Convert Word Documents to Clean HTML** – Easily converts text files to be published to HTML content with the same formatting – free - https://word2cleanhtml.com/

68. **Quick Sprout** – Connect your Google Analytics account with Quick Sprout and grow your website's traffic – free - https://www. quicksprout.com/

Facebook Analysis

69. **Wolfram|Alpha** – get a detailed Facebook report of your page or profile – free - http://www.wolframalpha.com/facebook/

70. **LikeAlyzer**– Measure and analyze the effectiveness of your Face- book pages – free - http://likealyzer.com/

71. **Fanpage Karma** – Get insights of your Facebook page to engage fans better – free for one page - https://www.fanpagekarma.com/

72. **Barometer** – Get a detailed performance report of your Facebook pages and posts – free - http://barometer.agorapulse.com/

Twitter Analysis

73. **SavePublishing** – Detect tweetable phrases with a single click – free - http://www.savepublishing.com/

74. **Tweriod** – Increase effectiveness of tweets by posting at the right time – free - http://www.tweriod.com/

75. **Mentionmapp** – Stay in updated with latest tweets and hashtags on twitter – free - http://mentionmapp.com/

76. **ManageFlitter** – a Twitter management tool – free - https://man- ageflitter.com/pro

77. **TweetDeck** – a social media dashboard to manage twitter accounts free - https://tweetdeck.twitter.com/

78. **The Latest** – Get notifications of the latest news and links links on twitter to – free - http://latest.is/

Visitor Activity and Heat maps

79. **Must Be Present** – Get a detailed engagement report of all your social profiles – free - https://mustbepresent.com/

80. **Mixpanel** – A digital footprint monitor for all devices – free - https://mixpanel.com/

81. **Inspectlet** - Records visitor sessions on your website and reports their activity pattern – free - https://www.inspectlet.com/

82. **Mouseflow** – Monitor visitor's navigation on your website – free - https://mouseflow.com/

83. **Crazy Egg** – its heat map and scroll map reports help understand your website visitors – free - https://www.crazyegg.com/

Live Website Chat

84. Zendesk Chat – Connect with your visitors in real time – free for 1 account - https://www.zopim.com/

85. SalesIQ – Live chat software – free trial - https://www.zoho.com/ salesiq/

E-commerce Software

86. Magento – Enhance visitor shopping experience – free - https:// magento.com/

87. Opencart – Add a checkout cart to your website for a seamless shopping experience of your visitors – free - https://www.opencart. com/

88. osCommerce – Sell your services and products securely by setting up an online store – free - http://www.oscommerce. com/

89. Zen Cart – open source shopping cart software – free - http://www. zen-cart.com/

90. CubeCart – e-commerce solution for your website – free - https:// www.cubecart.com/

Domain Appraisal

91. Estibot – Appraise your domain by better search engine ranking free with limitations -https://www.estibot.com/

92. Appraisal – Domain appraisal tool for better search engine ranking free - http://domainindex.com/

Web and Social Analytical Tools

93. **Google Analytics** – a tool to analyze and track website traffic – Free - https://www.google.com/analytics/#?modal_active=none

94. **Hotjar** – collect user feedback to turn visitors into customers - Free for personal use - https://www.hotjar.com/

95. **Simply Measured** – Get social media insights – Free demo - https:// simplymeasured.com/

96. **Crowdfire** – A social analytics tool that increases your Instagram and Twitter's post reach – free -https://www.crowdfireapp.com/

97. **Cyfe** – an all-in-one dashboard app that helps in monitoring and analyzing data – free - http://www.cyfe.com/

98. **Google Mobile Friendly** – check your website for mobile friendliness – free - https://search.google.com/search-console/ mobile-friendly?utm_source=mft&utm_ medium=redirect&utm_ campaign=mft-redirect

99. **Maxymizely** – optimize website content and placement – free - https://maxymizely.com/

Website Evaluation and Tests

100. **WebpageFX** - Check the readability score of your website – Free - https://www.webpagefx.com/tools/read-able/

101. **Hemingway** – Simplify your website or blog content to make its interpretable by any reader – free - http://www.hemingwayapp. com/

102. **Pingdom Website Speed Tool** – Check your website's speed and responsiveness with detailed reports – free - http://tools. pingdom.com/fpt/

103. **After the Deadline** – Check writing errors of your web content and save editing time – free - http://www. afterthedeadline.com/

104. **Website Grader** – Grade your website against key metrics – free -https://website.grader.com/

105. **Grade My Website** –Get a free analysis of your website – free - http://www.grademywebsite.com/

106. **Down for Everyone or Just me?** – Monitor your website's downtime – free -http://downforeveryoneorjustme.com/

107. **StatusCake** – Check your website's uptime every 5 minutes – free -https://www.statuscake.com/

107. **Uptime Robot** –monitoring tool to check website's uptime, downtime and response time – free –https://uptimerobot.com/

10. **Five Second Test** – Test the first impression of your website – free -http://fivesecondtest.com/

110. **Readable** – find out how readable your content is – free - https:// readable.io/

About The Author

Philip Masiello is the founder of Hound Dog Digital Marketing Agency, one of the fastest growing marketing agencies in the nation. The firm specializes in assisting consumer product companies with their E-commerce efforts, mobile application marketing and Amazon Seller marketing

But Mr. Masiello is also known as being the founder and CEO of several disruptive business models.

Prior to Hound Dog Digital Marketing, Mr. Masiello was a Founder and CEO of 800razors.com, an E-commerce company selling high quality American made razors and shaving products for men and women that compare in quality to the national brands at a fraction of the price. Some of the investors in 800razors.com were John Sculley, David Sculley and Michael Phelps. During this time, Mr. Masiello advised on the marketing of Mr. Sculley's personal web site, book, and learning series. He also advised on the marketing of Wolfgang Pucks's Online Cooking School.

Prior to 800razors.com, Mr. Masiello co-founded Raw Beauty, Inc. with Carol Alt, which developed and marketed Raw Essentials Skin Care through its web site, home shopping channels, and retailers worldwide. During this period, Mr. Masiello also assisted Forbes Riley, Nick Verreos and Marla Wynne in marketing their various fashion lines on HSN and Macy's stores and outlets.

Prior to Co-founding Raw Beauty, Inc., Mr. Masiello was a founder and President of Metro Marketing, an agency focused on developing the online, retail, and TV Shopping sales channels for emerging natural and organic brands.

Mr. Masiello also founded The Daily Market, a Washington, DC- based grab-and-go meal chain that was sold to a major supermarket chain. Mr. Masiello's first startup was at the age of 25.

Mr. Masiello holds an MBA in Finance and Marketing from the University of Maryland. He has remained active in the university's entrepreneurial programs and is also an active advisor and mentor to several incubators in the Baltimore/ Washington Marketplace.